Torch in the Night

Worship Resources from
South Africa

Anne Hope

Friendship Press • New York

The Center of Concern • Washington, D.C.

LIBRARY OF CONGRESS
Library of Congress Cataloging-in-Publication Data

Torch in the night: worship resources from South Africa / Anne Hope.
  p. cm.
  ISBN 0-3377-001822-1 : $5.95
  1. Liturgies. 2. Apartheid—South Africa—Meditation. I. Hope, Anne, 1930-.
BV198.T67 1988   87-36744
264--dc19   CIP

Unless otherwise stated, all Bible quotations in this book are from the
Revised Standard Version, copyright 1946 and 1952 by the Division of
Christian Education of the National Council of the Churches of Christ
in the United States of America. Quotations have in certain instances been
edited for inclusive language according to that organization's guidelines.

ISBN 0-377-00182-1
Friendship Press is the publishing house of the Division of Education
and Ministry of the National Council of the Churches of Christ in the
U.S.A. Editorial Offices: 475 Riverside Drive, Room 772, New York, NY
10115; Distribution Offices: P.O. Box 37844, Cincinnati, OH 45222-0844.

The Center of Concern is a non-profit, independent, interdisciplinary team
engaged in social analysis, policy advocacy and public education on issues
of justice and peace. Offices: 3700 13th Street, N.E., Washington, D.C. 20017.

This book is dedicated to Joan and Jimmy Stewart, who loved deeply the people and the poetry of South Africa, who founded the Transformation Center in Lesotho, and lived and died in deep commitment to the vision of a new future in southern Africa.

When the day comes on which our victory
    will shine like a torch in the night,
    it will be like a dream.
We will laugh and sing for joy.
Then the other nations will say about us,
    "The Lord did great things for them."
Indeed, he is doing great things for us;
that is why we are happy in our suffering.

Lord, break the chains of humiliation and death,
    just as on that glorious morning
    when you were raised.
Let those who weep as they sow the seeds of justice and
    freedom,
gather the harvest of peace and reconciliation.

Those who weep as they go out as instruments of your love
    will come back singing with joy,
    as they will manifest the disappearance of hate
and the manifestation of your love in your world.

—Psalm 126 as paraphrased by the
Rev. Zephania Kameeta
from *Why, O Lord? Psalms and Sermons
from Namibia*

Acknowledgements

I would like to give very special thanks to:

—Alicia Klein, for all her research in the Library of Congress finding poems not easily available in the United States of America

—Lucien Chauvin, for typing the entire manuscript onto discs and undertaking the difficult task of obtaining permission to use the material from authors and previous publishers

—Sally Timmel, for helping with the painful task of cutting when we had far more excellent material than could be included in this short book

and to all the staff of the Center of Concern.

Contents

Introduction

When we open our eyes and hearts to the suffering caused by apartheid, South Africa seems like a country in the dark of "night . . . hideous night." So the present time is described by Mongane Serote, one of South Africa's greatest poets. Yet even in the darkest of nights one sees the stars, and as Serote says, "The night keeps winking . . . the stars keep whistling and whistling . . . whispering and whispering."

For those who live in that darkness, the faith that God is on the side of the poor and oppressed and that, finally, victory is certain, is like "a torch in the night." Throughout the long struggle for freedom and the long years of endurance there has been constant activity as people learn "how to make a day." Much courage has shone forth from men and women unknown and famous, young and old. This courage, too, is for us like "a torch in the night" as we face a wider world where many of the same patterns exist, even if they are less sharply defined. So as we enter into the darkness of sin and suffering in South Africa let us also celebrate the light in the darkness: the faith, the heroism, the courage not only of a few leaders, but of hundreds of thousands of unknown people.

Times of intense struggle for revolutionary change are often times of great artistic creativity. The human spirit seems to assert itself in spite of devastating conditions, harnessing all its energies in an extraordinary outpouring of poetry, storytelling, drama, music and dance, art and photography—expressions of people's commitment to transformative action.

Over the last twenty years a surge of cultural activity has accompanied the South African people's determination to win their freedom. Different groups are expressing themselves in different ways: Young people are writing poetry. Women are telling their stories; those who have had little opportunity for formal education describe their lives in response to questions in lively interviews. Three outstanding women leaders, Ellen Kuzwayo, Helen Joseph and Winnie Mandela have written autobiographies, drawing together the strands of history, enlivening the story of the struggle with anecdotes of famous leaders. The men of the older generation

i

give speeches and sermons. Some have given testimony of their deepest convictions in famous court trials, where, though they were in the dock, it was always the government of South Africa that was on trial. Meanwhile, dramatists, both those preparing polished productions and those creating street and "guerrilla" theatre, use irony and humor to help the community deal with its humiliation and pain.

If we believe that God is revealed not only in the written Scriptures but also in the experience of the human heart and in the history of the human race, the stories, poems, dramas and works of art of such a moment in time can be sources of inspiration for us. For they offer a way to understand not only the life and experience of people in a particular time and place, but also a way to encounter for ourselves both the grandeur of the human spirit and the always unpredictable actions of the living God.

How to use the book

The poems and stories in this book can be read in silence and solitude, but they are far more powerful when read aloud in a prayerful gathering, at a protest meeting or in celebration. As we read and hear them we join with Christians all over the world who are involved in "contextual" theology. This means that instead of starting with God's revelation in Scripture and seeing how it affects our lives, a Christian community starts out by reflecting on its own experience of life. It asks, what is God communicating through this experience? and then determines what light is shed by related biblical passages. Since South Africa brings into clear focus patterns of inequality that exist between the first and the third world in many other regions, the reflections that arise from these readings can be as challenging for North Americans as for South Africans.

The readings are arranged in chapters according to theme. Each chapter includes suggestions for designing a "ritual," a time of worship intended to illuminate that theme. Since a group using this book might consist of a few friends sitting around a fire or a church full of people, it is not practical to give detailed instructions on how to conduct each ritual. Instead, suggestions are made for Scripture readings; for simple, symbolic actions; and for questions to help participants draw parallels with their own experience and to motivate their own personal reflection.

For most of the rituals, a large candle (a "torch") is placed in the center of the room, surrounded by elements appropriate to the theme of the readings. The session begins with the lighting of the candle as a reminder of God's presence among us and in our world. Then, for a few moments, all other lights are turned out as participants prepare to be present to both the darkness and the light. After a moment of silence, a few lines of poetry or the introduction to the chapter is read. Then the lights are turned on again and the group proceeds with other readings and the symbolic action.

A few guidelines to keep in mind while planning the rituals:

1. Give readings to the readers well in advance to allow them time to prepare. A reader needs to develop empathy with the poet or writer. Timing and pace are crucial. A rehearsal may be well worth the time, especially if a selection will be read before a large group, or if it is a choral or dramatic reading.

2. Display photographs around the room to bring the South African situation to life. Plan a time of silent prayer during which people can look at the photos. Ask each person to choose one of the faces in the photos and to stand quietly before it, trying to imagine what that individual's life must be like. With a smaller group, a book of photographs can be passed around before the readings begin. Some of the books of photographs listed under Resources on page 131 can be borrowed from your local library.

3. Music can make a great difference in a ritual. Use tapes of South African music as well as North American music that is popular in South Africa. See Resources.

4. Audiovisuals can greatly enhance understanding of South Africa. Show appropriate filmstrips, videos and films whenever possible. See Resources.

5. The symbolic actions are intended to help people move from an intellectual to a prayerful experience. These should be performed quietly and reverently. Music may be used in the background. If a group is not used to such a symbolic action, it should be introduced by an experienced leader who knows how to establish an atmosphere of prayer; soon, others may share this role.

6. Sharing leadership is important; as many people as possible should be encouraged to take an active role: reading, contributing to a spontaneous litany, composing a short prayer or blessing.

7. If there are more than eight people in the group it would be best to divide into groups of three for discussion or shared reflection.

Mother and Child

The woodcuts reprinted on pages iv, 32, 35, 52, 78, 81, 99, 108 and 120 are by South African artist Azaria Mbatha, now living in exile in Sweden. Using symbols from the Zulu tradition, Mbatha's art gives "expression to the suffering of those people in South Africa who are at the mercy of the mighty. . ." In the example above, the young mother in the upper part of the picture "has decorated her fence with masks bearing the features of her ancestors to show that she is calling for their help. She is worried about her child." These pictures are reprinted, with the artist's permission, from his book, In the Heart of the Tiger (Im Hertzen des Tigers). *Wuppertal, Federal Republic of Germany: Vereinigte Evangelische Mission, 1986.*

1. Children Under Apartheid

In any unjust society those who are most vulnerable—the very young and the very old—always suffer the most. Such is certainly the case in apartheid South Africa. For decades, children's lives have been made bitterly painful by laws and employment patterns that break up family life and shatter the security of early childhood; by intensely overcrowded housing in urban areas, which puts additional stress on family relationships; by hunger, malnutrition and grinding poverty; and by parents' frequent unemployment.

Throughout much of South Africa the winters are bitterly cold; many children have few clothes. Traditionally, from a very early age boys have looked after the sheep and goats, work that becomes a double hardship when it deprives them of education. Very young girls often look after their younger brothers and sisters and do all the housework while their mothers, usually the family's sole breadwinners, go out to work. Yet here, as all over Africa, most adults warmly love not only their own children but all the children in the community.

The poems that begin this chapter celebrate the birth of a baby yet agonize over the pain of bringing a child into the South African situation. Some of the poems offer a glimpse of the irrepressible delight just in being alive that every child experiences at times. Following these brief joys we hear children's haunting questions, growing frustrations and anger at parents for allowing South Africa's dehumanizing situation to continue so long. Finally we hear their determination to take the future into their own hands no matter what the cost.

Ritual

Life is often symbolized as light. Prepare a centerpiece with a large

1

candle surrounded by candleholders for several small candles. Place fresh greenery, such as ivy or pine boughs showing fresh, new life around the candles. Use music to create a quiet atmosphere. Then, lighting the large candle, call people's attention to the presence of God in and among them, with all those they know and with all the people of the world. Ask them to reflect for a few moments on the first time they can remember feeling glad to be alive. Give each person a minute to share this memory with a person next to him or her. Then ask everyone to turn their minds to the children of South Africa, and to recall silently all they know about what life is like for them. Turn out the lights as people become aware of the darkness and pain in the lives of South Africa's children. After a few minutes, turn on the lights again. Read the introduction to this chapter and the poems that follow. After each poem, light one of the small candles from the main candle and place it in a holder. Each small candle represents the life of a child, unique and infinitely precious.

Scripture: Matthew 2:13-18. The Massacre of the Babies of Bethlehem.

Children are often innocent victims in situations of greed, domination and structural injustice all over the world. Ask participants to give examples of this. Each time an example is given, extinguish one of the small candles. Let the center candle remain lit.

Questions:
- Do we really believe that God is always there?
- How can we make sense of the suffering of the innocent?
- To what action does this suffering call us? (Possibilities for action are suggested in *South Africa's Moment of Truth*, by Edgar Lockwood. See inside back cover for ordering information.)

End the ritual with spontaneous prayer and/or the following closing prayer:

O God, Creator and Artist, Mother and Father,
You fill the eyes and hearts of children
with laughter and love
with twinkling mischief and abounding curiosity.
We see them brimming with hope
secure in an unspoken promise
that life is a blessing;
that your world and your people are good.

Forgive us for all the ways in which we have betrayed the children.
Too many babies die before they are one year old;

2

Too many, before they are five,
experience hunger, weakness,
avoidable disease and death.
Too many soon look out on the world
with the round, bewildered eyes of fear and disappointment.
Forgive us that we have cared more about profits than about people,
about gaining gold than guarding the children.

Empower us all to know and use our power;
Give us guidance and understanding
to see clearly what we can do
to ensure that no child is hungry or thirsty,
and that fathers and mothers are not forced to abandon their children
in order to earn their daily bread.

We ask this in the name of Jesus our Lord,
who loved children.

Readings

The Soweto Child

Swimming and frolicking
in primordial waters
the Embryo
soon will cry Oh, this beautiful this harsh world

Opening eyes
opening nostrils
hearing harmonies and confused noises
Sermons of love drowned by bursts of hate

The waters break forth
then cease their flowing

And the Embryo emerges
crown, forehead, ears
eyes to see for itself
this beautiful this harsh world
Then shoulders and chest
and waist and loins
thighs, knees, calves, ankles
and feet to tread upon this

soft as down
earth this
gritty as gravel
earth
And there's a splitting yell
  Oh, what's this place
  Where am I?
As umbilical cord snaps

Sing for me a lullaby mother
a lullaby mother a lullaby mother
Sing for me a lullaby mother
and let me rest in the warmth of your lap
Sing for me a war-song comrades
a war-song comrades a war-song comrades
Sing for me a war-song comrades
let's rush to the field of the circling crow

Then one hand upon the tender breast
the other flinging stinging barbs
And the monster limps
and the assembled hosts shout
Yebo! Mgwaze! Yebo! Mgwaze!
seeing the barbarous monster tottering

In this harsh
this beautiful
world.

           —Daniel P. Kunene
           from *A Seed Must Seem to Die*

Mother's Ode to a Stillborn Child

You languished patiently
for months on end
in dungeon darkness
in intestinal convolutions
and indefinable chaos

You had neither shadow
nor silhouette
You had every right
to riot and complain
or raise your voice
in protest or defiance

I could feel your lust
to join the dead
living world
Your muted attempts
to burst like a Christmas chicken
into life

It is not my fault
that you did not live
to be a brother sister
or lover of some black child
that you did not experience pain
pleasure voluptuousness and salt
in the wound
that your head did not stop
a police truncheon
that you are not a permanent resident
of a prison island.

—Mandlenkosi Langa
from *To Whom It May Concern*

The Shepherd and His Flock

The rays of the sun
are like a pair of scissors
cutting the blanket
of dawn from the sky.

The young shepherd
drives the master's sheep

from the paddock
into the veld.*
His bare feet
kick the grass
and spill the dew
like diamonds
on a cutter's table.

A lamb strays away
enchanted by the marvels
of a summer morning;
the ram
rebukes the ewe,
"Woman! Woman!
Watch over the child!"

The sun wings up
on flaming petals
of a sunflower.

He perches on an antheap
to play the reed flute,
and to salute
the farmer's children
going to school,
and dreamily asks,
"O! Wise Sun above,
will you ever guide
me into school?"

—Oswald J. Mtshali
from *Sounds of a Cowhide Drum*

I Will Wait

I have tasted, ever so often,
Hunger like sand on my tongue
And tears like flames have licked my eye-lids

* Uncultivated grasslands

Blurring that which I want to see,
I want to know.
But Oh! often, now and then, everywhere I have been,
Joy, real as paths,
Has spread within me like pleasant scenery,
Has run beneath my flesh like rivers glitteringly silver;
And now I know:
Having been so flooded and so dry,
I wait.

—Mongane Wally Serote
from *To Whom It May Concern*

Boy on a Swing

Slowly he moves
to and fro, to and fro,
then faster and faster
he swishes up and down.
His blue shirt
billows in the breeze
like a tattered kite.

The world whirls by:
east becomes west,
north turns to south;
the four cardinal points
meet in his head.

Mother!
Where did I come from?
When will I wear long trousers?
Why was my father jailed?

—Oswald Mtshali
from *Sounds of a Cowhide Drum*

Solar Power

Sitting in the sun
in the dust
little blanket over tiny shoulders
happiness being
the warmth of the winter sun

Winter sun
respite from blistering cold
chilling wind
howling at night
raising dust at day

Winter sun
respite only

When the summer has arrived
I will throw off my tattered blanket
give my body wholly to the sun
to warm
to heal
to restore

—Daniel P. Kunene
from *A Seed Must Seem to Die*

Naked They Come*

I have seen them come,
At break-neck speed,
Beheading wild flowers,
With kicks from serrated edges
Of naked black feet,
As naked they come.

* When a train stops in a rural area, hungry, begging children seem to appear from nowhere.

Pot-bellied, bow-legged,
They jump as they come,
A scourge on my conscience
For poverty is their blanket,
Bought from one common shop,
The shop of inheritance.

Naked they come,
With complete abandon,
All sizes, all ages,
They stand and they gaze,
What a sight!
A tourist attraction.

Their lives insured,
Yes, unquestionably safe,
For soon they will join,
To work on the mines,
To work on the farms,
And soon more will come,
For naked they come.
Perhaps a crumb,
From my impoverished hand,
Will stem their hunger,

And crush their pride,
Of people in their land,
The land of their birth,
For naked they come,
To their real homeland.

—Basil Somhlahlo
from *To Whom It May Concern*

Soweto

A dialogue between a twelve-year-old girl and death

"The child was twelve years old, if that. She was wearing her
school uniform. In the eyes of the South African police, she was
not a child She was one of a mass of anonymous, faceless blacks

9

she lay in the street, dying."

Where am I? Why am I lying here in the dust?

> *O, child of a woman, how can I speak the unspeakable to a mere twelve-year-old? Isn't that the problem?*

Who are you? Where are you? Speak to me. Hold me tight.
My mother does not know I'm lying here in the dusty street.

> *O, child of a woman, I am and I am not, for I come after the final darkness has closed in.*

Darkness? What are you saying?

> *Quiet. Just rest a while, child of a man and a woman, seed of the sacred union. Do not worry, little girl.*

Seed of the sacred union?
> *You cannot understand.*

Mother.

> *She cannot hear you, O child. You do not know what is becoming of you.*

She will come, my mother. She will hear me. She will come.

> *I have no comfort for you, O unfortunate child, barely twelve years old. I am now your only companion.*

Touch me, I'm hot.

> *No.*

My head is whirling. Hold me.

> *No.*

Please, you thing.

> *Yes, I am thing and I am no-thing. I must stay away from you ʌs long as possible.*

Can you go to my mother and tell her. . .?

> *I cannot.*

Oh, I'm tired. I'm drowsy.

> *Sleep. That dust now is hallowed ground, where you lie.*

It comes back now. I was walking. Yes. From school.
My books, where are they? What happened to me? Why am I here? Oh, mother.

> *Do not linger long, child. Be released. Let me embrace you.*

Please.

Not now.

This dryness in my mouth. I'm thirsty. Mother, bring me some water.

(I am merciful.)

Then bring me water.

O, you heard me. That was not for you, child. How merciful I am you will, mercifully, never know.

There were many people. Policemen. Guns . . . They shot me! Oh, mother they shot me! Shot . . . me.
Why?

Because they feared you.

Feared me? Me, a child? Those big, big men with guns and clubs and bayonets? Feared me?

In you, a child, more strength. You to them a greater threat in the young tomorrows waiting to be born. They fear your tomorrow, that's why they try to kill you today. You understand?

Blood! I'm bleeding! They shot me!

Out of fear, child. But your tomorrow will never die. For, when I embrace you, you will live in the endlessness of time, in all the yester-days, the todays and the tomorrows which will become one thing.

My mother kissed me this morning. She left for the white people's house to go and cook for them and wash their clothes and care for their children. She said she'd see me in the evening. I ate. I left. I loved the arithmetic. Good subject. The teacher, he is good. English. Hygiene—wash every day, brush your teeth, comb your hair, cut your nails short. Civics—who is your Bantu Affairs Commissioner? Who is the superintendent of your location? In what ways is the pass good for you? That piece of paper which the policemen are always demanding from you, without which they throw you in jail! Oh, how our people suffer!

Don't tire yourself, little one. So young. So beautiful! So tender! Just lie there and rest and wait. Your tomorrow will never die.

Afrikaans! Why in hell! Why-y-y? Comrades, they shot me.
Yes, the cowards! They shot me. But I hear your running feet, I hear your call to arms. I see victory! See how I pull myself up from the dust! See how I clench my fist! See how I make the final salute!

I hear the shout "TO HELL" echoing in the four corners of the earth! Yes, to hell with them! To hell with them! . . .
Oh, mother, will you know when you see my happy face that my heart remains here with my comrades? With you? Tomorrow is so beautiful!

> *Tomorrow shall be born, for today is indestructible. No sun sets forever. You, child, are like a seed that must seem to die in order to produce a young shoot seven days hence.*

Tomorrow is ours!

> *Brave child! You're like a meteor that blazes and lights the earth ere it is extinguished. The straying traveller sees the way and is saved. The child, let meteor trail off to silence, deep silence, well-earned silence, peace.*

Tomorrow lives! Soweto! Soweto! So . . . we . . . to . . . So . . . we . . .
> *Now you're ready for my embrace. Come, little one. It is finished.*

—Daniel P. Kunene
from *A Seed Must Seem to Die*

Ishmael (14 years)

The drawings on page 12 and 21 are reprinted with permission from **Two Dogs and Freedom: Black Children of South Africa Speak Out** *(New York: Rosset and Company, Inc., 1987).*

2. The Rise of the Angry Generation

The children have arrived.
From them we must learn to create the unending movement.
By their birth we must swim through the turbulence like a bird.
Our peace is born from their innocence.
It is a song that praises the earth.

—Mazisi Kunene
from *The Ancestors and the Sacred Mountain*

"Ever since the Soweto revolt in 1976, black children in South Africa have been at the cutting edge of their country's history. They began by protesting against an inadequate and racist educational system and, in subsequent years, fought on a broader front for political change that would both stiffen the resolve of their elders and lead to the transformation of the society in which they were trapped. There are few countries in the world, at any time in history, where children have found themselves so much in the front line of a determined and violent struggle for change, or where so much historical weight has been placed on such young shoulders."

"Children on the Front Line"
1987 UNICEF Report

Ritual

This prayer service should be held around a fire, either a bonfire outdoors or a fireplace in a living room. Even in a meeting room it is possible to make a small fire in a metal disk, as is often done in Roman Catholic churches for the Easter vigil. Have a pile of small pieces of wood ready by the fire. Jesus said, "I came to cast fire upon the earth; and would that it were already kindled!" (Luke 12:49-50)

Fire is a symbol of power and of the transformation of power. It brings light and warmth. It transforms dead wood into dancing energy. It destroys rubble, melts what is cold and hard and purifies as it burns. Fire is also dangerous. There is fire in South Africa now. Fire reminds us that anger, which is often a good and necessary source of energy, can easily change into destructive hostility and hatred.

If the group is indoors, turn out the lights for a minute and let people reflect on the fire in South Africa. Then turn the lights back on and read the introduction to this chapter and the poems and excerpts. Pause from time to time and ask someone to put another piece of wood on the fire. While he or she is doing this, pray both in thanksgiving and in supplication for the fire that is in young South Africans. Pray that it may be a transforming flame, destroying what is evil, but also overcoming hostility and hatred.

Scripture: Choose one of the following three passages:

1) Matthew 18:1-7,10. Jesus takes a child and sets the child in their midst. "Whoever causes one of these little ones who believe in me to sin, it would be better for him to have a great millstone fastened round his neck and to be drowned in the depth of the sea."
• What would Jesus say about our world today where children suffer so much?

2) 1 Samuel 17:1-52. The story of David and Goliath. (This is a favorite reading with many Christian groups in Africa as they struggle against overwhelming power and arrogance.)
• In what situations do we feel small and powerless?
• What difference does it make to our work and witness if we have faith that God is on the side of the poor and oppressed?

3) John 2:13-17. Jesus drives the moneychangers from the temple.
• When is anger a positive and appropriate reaction to a situation?
• What are we really angry about?
• Do we use the energy aroused by our anger in the struggle for justice?
• How can we channel our anger toward constructive change and avoid hostility and hatred?

Even if you chose the first or second Scripture reading, ask the questions following the third reading as well, so that as participants watch the fire they can think about their own anger and how they

14

use the energy it generates. Keep some of the ashes for the following ritual.

Action: Find out from one of the North American groups doing advocacy work (see *South Africa's Moment of Truth*) whether there are still children held in detention in South Africa. If so, send postcards to President Botha asking for their immediate release.

End the ritual with the poem "The Child Who Was Shot Dead by Soldiers at Nyanga."

Readings

The Rise of the Angry Generation

The great eagle lifts its wings from the dream
And the shells of childhood are scattered
Letting the fierce eyes focus on the morning
As though to cover the earth with darkness.
The beautiful bird builds its nest with old leaves
Preparing the branches of the birth-plant
Covering them with red feathers
As though to warn the earth against its anger.
The once proud planet shrieks in terror
Opening a vast space for the mysterious young bird
For the merciless talons of the new generation
They who are not deterred by false tears
Who do not turn away from the fire
They are the children of iron
They are the fearless bees of the night
They are the wrath of the volcanic mountains
They are the abiding anger of the Ancestral Forefathers.

> —Mazisi Kunene
> from *The Ancestors and the Sacred Mountain*

June 16, 1976

"The children picked up stones, they used dustbin lids as shields and marched towards machine guns. It's not that they don't know that the white man is heavily armed; they marched against heavy machine gun fire. You could smell gunfire everywhere. Children were dying in the street, and as they were dying, the others marched forward, facing guns. No one has ever underestimated the power of the enemy. We know that he is armed to the teeth. But the determination, the thirst for freedom in children's hearts, was such that they were prepared to face those machine guns with stones. That is what happens when you hunger for freedom, when you want to break those chains of oppression. Nothing else seems to matter.

—Winnie Mandela
from *Part of My Soul Went with Him*

Warrior

Trash-can lid
  for shield
Stone
  for bullet
Arm
  for propulsion
Mere child besides

True shield
  That's in the heart
True bullet
  That's in the heart
True propulsion
  That's in the heart
True man
True woman
  That's in the heart

Ten times ten
Tons
of
TNT
Are the ripeness she feels inside of her
This is the Soweto Child

—Daniel Kunene
from *A Seed Must Seem to Die*

Wednesday, 18 August 1976

What a miserable weekend. We went to church in the morning but no one would say a word about all that's happening because we have this informer, Jason, in our congregation. We know he's an informer because he's tried to get others to join up. In the afternoon we went to see the family of that boy I saw in the hospital Thursday night but they already knew of his whereabouts.

I had quite a shock later. Arthur came to tell me that the schoolboy who was shot at Langa was one of the Mosi family, Xolile.* I know his brother and his family well. Xolile was a student at Langa High. His mother is alone here as the father is somewhere in the country. They stay in one of those shacks in Elsies River. She can't get a house in Guguletu because her stay here is not legal. The funeral is on Saturday.

There are several stories of what happened. One person there said Xolile was armed with a short axe and charged an African policeman. It was an African who shot him. Others say he opened his shirt and just ran at them shouting, "Well, if you have got my friend, then take me too." So they shot him at point-blank range, because one of the girls behind him was hit by the same bullet. Who knows? I suppose they felt he was asking for it.

The children are really organized now. They meet every day. Langa High is the gathering point. The newspapers are saying that school attendance is up but that is nonsense. These children are not attending classes. They are only there for the meetings to decide what action to take next. I hear they spent Sunday going from church to church collecting up bail and for the funerals of the Mosi boy and another who went to Intshinga. At the Langa Baptist Church alone they got R 26. . . .

They are wearing their uniforms all week now, even on Sundays, because the police are denying that the Mosi boy was a student. They've decided the police must shoot them in their uniforms.

—Diary of Maria Tholo
from "A Day of Funerals" in *A Land Apart*

---

* X, as in *Xolile* or *Xhosa*, is a lateral "click" sound. Most non-Xhosa speakers pronounce it as a hard *k*.

The school boycott continues

The simmering unrest in Soweto and the boycott of black schools in many areas had persisted into 1977. The spirit of the students and the school children had not been broken by the horrors of 1976, the hundreds of dead, imprisoned, injured, detained[*].

Throughout the year, the long boycott continued and spread, deepening in intensity. Some five hundred African school teachers and principals resigned their teaching posts in support of the students' stand. "A headmaster without pupils is irrelevant," said one principal. . . .

Detaining the leaders for six months in 1976 had not helped to subdue the unrest. Even police violence and intimidation could not force the children into the schools. The boycott was spreading both ways, upwards into the black universities and downwards into primary schools. Small children knew about "boycott" even if they didn't always understand what it was all about. My small black godson would refuse to put on his shoes, saying, "Boycott, no school today, mum." He was five years old.

—Helen Joseph
from *Side by Side*

Notes

Yesterday when the sun was falling
and there was no moon
nor stars
when the night was dark
remember
the glitter in the eyes of children
which shone and shone
shone like the glow of death in the eyes of the old and dying
remember
the nights
when the snare of spider-webs
dangled from our eyelashes, finger and toes
and we lived lives of a land of drought
we looked at each other then
knowing lots about hopelessness
yet

[*] Arrested without trial

18

knowing also
that the night was no good for us
and that our day must come
remember
how in hopelessness
a secret was hatched
a secret which now changes our walk and our sight
for we know what makes a day
a day is not made by time only
nor by praying
nor by wishing—this we know
a day is made by us
when we will it, when we carry the night through
how?
I ask Steve
and I ask Solomon
how do we do that
I ask
I ask the night which gave birth to a red day
June 16
remember
when we learnt how to trip a hippo* in the night
and declared to the world
our will to be free
a secret hatched in the thick of the night
a night with no moon nor stars
a night which we
a people
who know that life has strength,
that life can carry a heavy night,
here we are now
and we have transformed the night. . .
listen
only if you listen can you hear footsteps
rolling quietly like the clouds
one day
when the day comes
and the night moonless and starless

* Army vehicle

19

is dragged and is gone
we shall sing a song
a song
which transforms
the misery of the millions
the millions who starved
a song
remember
how in love of freedom wave after wave after wave
building strength after strength
rolling and rolling time after time
crushing and crushing
a song
in life and action
breaking the night and building a day
when we will live free
to work and build our land.

—Mongane Wally Serote
from *The Night Keeps Winking*

The Child Who Was Shot Dead by Soldiers at Nyanga

The child is not dead
The child lifts his fist against his mother
who shouts Afrika! shouts the breath
of freedom and the veld
in the locations of the cordoned heart

The child lifts his fist against his father
in the march of the generations
who shout Afrika! shout the breath
of righteousness and blood
in the streets of his embattled pride

The child is not dead
not at Langa nor at Nyanga
not at Orlando nor at Sharpeville
nor at the police station at Phillippi
where he lies with a bullet through his brain

The child is the dark shadow of the soldiers
on guard with rifles, saracens* and batons
the child is present at all assemblies and law-givings
the child peers through the windows of houses
    and into the hearts of mothers
this child who just wanted to play in the sun at Nyanga
    is everywhere
the child grown to a man treks through all of Africa
the child grown to a giant journeys through the whole world

Without a pass
                    —Ingrid Jonker
                    from *South Africa, The Cordoned Heart*

Gerald (13 years)

* Army vehicles

3. Years of Repression

Exploitation of Africans, Indians and so-called "Coloureds" began long before the Afrikaner Nationalists came to power in 1948, but the laws of the 1950s, 60s and 70s entrenched the poverty and suffering of the vast majority of black people. Any attempt to change the power structure has met with ruthless repression. The result has been the development of a vast and sophisticated system of control based on a network of informers, police, prisons and military strength. The policy reinforcing this system is one of "divide and rule." Using carefully calculated plans, the South African government creates disunity among blacks and fosters ethnic and class animosity by co-opting and corrupting a few privileged individuals and groups. The government has also attempted to crush every effort to build unity and effective organization by banishing leaders to remote rural areas; by deporting, exiling, arresting and detaining, often without trial, those who have shown leadership; and by banning many others from social contact and educational and political activities.

Ritual

Light the candle and turn out the lights for a few moments of silent reflection in the darkness.

> The night is silent with experience,
>   this night
> in these parts of the world. . . .
>   —Mongane Serote

Turn the lights on again.

We have kept some of the ashes from the fire used in the last ritual. Ash is a very ancient symbol of penitence. In the Old Testament, even King David repented wearing sackcloth and ashes.

Ash Wednesday services marking the beginning of Lent are based on this symbol.

As we listen to readings about South Africa's long years of repression and struggle, let us remember that the present regime could never have survived without the support of the western world. (For more background, see *South Africa's Moment of Truth*, especially Chapter Five.) Invite the group to reflect on its own involvement in structures that perpetuate repression, and on people's silence and apathy in the face of oppressive structures around the world. Ask the participants to name some of these (e.g., the arms race, taxes used for military aid, the debt crisis in the third world).

Each time someone speaks, she or he goes to the dish of ashes and marks a cross with ashes on his or her forehead, chin or hands. Give everyone an opportunity to do this, even if they do not wish to speak. Applying ashes may be a depressing act, but the prophets of the Bible promise that if we repent, God will grant us new life. As we focus our attention on the gospel as good news for the poor and oppressed, let us remember the story of the phoenix, the bird that rises resplendent from the ashes of its own burnt nest.

Scripture: Luke 4:16-21. "He has anointed me to preach good news to the poor."

This text has probably been used more frequently than any other by Christians committed to the struggle for justice, especially in Africa, Latin America and Asia. It is the basis on which they interpret the gospel as Good News.

- How does the South African situation help us to realize more fully the significance of this scriptural text?
- What are its implications for North American Christians?
- What do you think when you hear "Good News is Bad News, is Good News," the title of a book on liberation theology for North Americans?

Close with the Confession of Sins on page 34 and the hymn, "He Sent Me to Bring Good News to the Poor"* or another appropriate hymn.

Readings

The Politician and the Priest

Alan Paton was one of the first authors to reveal the sufferings of blacks

---

* Available in the hymnal *Glory and Praise*, Vol. I, North American Liturgy Resources, 10802 N. 23rd Avenue, Phoenix, AZ 85029.

to white South Africans and to the wider world in his 1948 novel, Cry, The Beloved Country. *Many aspects of life in South Africa have not changed since then; in fact, the callousness and cruelty with which apartheid laws have been applied has made the struggle for survival and the effort to live with those one loves even more difficult. This extract from a verse adaptation of Paton's book describes a conversation between John Kumalo, a black politician, and the Rev. Msimangu, a black Anglican priest. Kumalo begins:*

Here in Johannesburg it is the mines—
Everything is the mines.
This wonderful City Hall, this beautiful Parktown
With its beautiful houses—all this is built
with gold from the mines.
This wonderful hospital for Europeans,
The biggest hospital south of the Equator,
It is built with the gold from the mines. . . .
Go to our hospital,
And see our people lying on the floors.
They lie so close you cannot step over them.
But it is they who dig the gold.
For three shillings a day.
We come from the Transkei, and from Basutoland,
From Bechuanaland, Swaziland, Zululand.
And from Ndotsheni also.
We live in the compounds,
We must leave our wives and families behind.
And when new gold is found,
It is the white man's share that will rise.
They bring more of us to live in the compounds,
To dig under the ground for three shillings a day.
They do not think, Here is a chance to pay more for our labor.
They think, Here is a chance
To build a bigger house and buy a bigger car.
It is important to find gold, they say,
For all of South Africa is built on the mines.
But it is not built on the mines: it is built
On our backs, on our sweat, on our labor.
And what does a chief know about that?
The Bishop says it is wrong, but he lives

In a big house, and his white priests
Get four, five, six times what you get, my brother. . . .
That is why I no longer go to Church.

As Kumalo and Msimangu walk away, Msimangu says:
I have one great fear in my heart: that one day
When they are turned to loving, they will find we
Are turned to hating. . . .

　　　　　　—Felicia Komai
　　　　　　　from a verse adaptation of *Cry, the Beloved Country*

Taken for a Ride

The pass is the most hated symbol of oppression. It is a document permitting an African to be in an urban area. If found without it, a person is arrested and taken for a ride to jail in the kwela-kwela *(police van).*

I get my cue
from the glint in the cop's eye.
I have seen it before.
So I have to find it.

I pull away from Mono
and hug myself in desperation.
Up, down, back, front, sides,
like a crazed tribal dancer.
I have to find it.

Without it I'm lost, with it I'm lost,
a cipher in Albert Street.
I hate it. I nurse it,
my pass, my everything.

Up, down, back, front, sides,
Mono's lip twitches,
She looks at me with all the love.
She shakes her head nervously.
Up, front, sides, back, down,
like a crazed tribal dancer.
Molimo!*

* Lord

25

The doors of the kwela-kwela gape,
I jabber at Mono.
The doors swing lazy, sadistic like Jonah's whale.
I take a free ride.

> —Stanley Motjuwadi
> from *To Whom It May Concern*

The signing of the Freedom Charter at the congress at Kliptown, 1955

The congress was to be held on a football ground in Kliptown outside Johannesburg, adjacent to Soweto, as no hall would be large enough for this gathering. It had to be held in an area where all must be free to come, black and white. It was all rather primitive and very simple, but the people gave it dignity, the mass of people coming together to spell out their own freedom charter. There were too few seats and many of the delegates sat on the ground. The only structure was the speakers' platform, with the huge four-spoked wheel to represent the four organizations which made up the Congress Alliance. I was to be a speaker in the section dealing with houses, security and comfort. I felt greatly honored.

I watched the groups coming into the enclosure bearing banners, "Let us speak of Freedom!", "Let us go forward to Freedom!" They came from far and near; some had travelled all night in trucks or kombis*. Not every group had reached Kliptown, for the police had been busy stopping vehicles, on every possible traffic pretext, from continuing their journey.

I could feel the strength and the indomitable purpose of these people as they marched in. They had sent their demands ahead of them. There had been one thousand and more, sometimes only scraps of paper, sometimes formally set out. They had come to this congress to hear, to discuss and to adopt their own charter of the future, born of their heartaches and their hopes. It was a simple beginning for a charter which has proved indestructible, which refuses to die, despite sporadic bannings of sundry editions of it. A printed piece of paper can be banned, but not the ideas expressed in it.

The draft Freedom Charter was read to the congress and on Saturday and the next day, it was heard again.

. . . South Africa belongs to all who live in it, black and white!

* Volkswagon bus

26

... And we pledge ourselves to strive together, sparing neither strength nor courage, until the democratic changes here set out have been won.

THE PEOPLE SHALL GOVERN.
ALL NATIONAL GROUPS SHALL HAVE EQUAL RIGHTS.
THE PEOPLE SHALL SHARE IN THE COUNTRY'S WEALTH.
THE LAND SHALL BE SHARED AMONG THOSE WHO WORK IT.
ALL SHALL BE EQUAL BEFORE THE LAW.
ALL SHALL ENJOY EQUAL HUMAN RIGHTS.
THERE SHALL BE WORK AND SECURITY.
THE DOORS OF LEARNING AND CULTURE SHALL BE OPENED.
THERE SHALL BE HOUSES, SECURITY AND COMFORT.
THERE SHALL BE PEACE AND FRIENDSHIP.

These freedoms we will fight for, side by side, throughout our lives, until we have won our liberty.

The affirmations came over loud and clear as the delegates spoke of them, adopted them, and the draft charter began to take on a reality, moving forward, section by section, until there were only two sections left for discussion and adoption.

I was on the platform, the four-spoked congress wheel behind me, waiting to make my speech on houses, security and comfort. It was nearly four o'clock when I became aware of a stirring among the crowd. I saw that we were surrounded by armed police and a posse was moving towards the platform, a dozen or so detectives in plain clothes, escorted by police carrying stun guns.

The crowd seemed stunned, all eyes on the advancing police, who mounted the platform and presented the chairman with a warrant to investigate high treason. It seemed incredible, unreal, high treason at this gathering of peaceful people adopting a freedom charter. The chairman informed the delegates of the reason for the police invasion and asked if they wished to proceed with the congress. The crowd roared its assent and rose to its feet in a defiant "Nkosi Sikelele."[*]

I gave my speech, surrounded as we all were on the platform, by the armed policemen. The microphone had been damaged in the confusion. There was barely standing room for us and the policemen on the platform, but someone held the microphone wobbling in front of me. I saw police already working their way

* Nkosi Sikelil'i Afrika: "God Bless Africa." An unofficial black national anthem, used also in other African nations.

up and down the rows of delegates, searching as they went, opening bags, looking for documents, not weapons. The police had the weapons, not the people in the crowd.

As I spoke, I looked at the people, three thousand of them, seated in front of me, so many bright headscarves, so many people proudly displaying the black, green and yellow of the ANC [African National Congress] colors. They were indifferent to the searching police, as if they had been tiresome insects. They were no longer watching them, their eyes were on their leaders and I realized, almost unbelieving, that they were in fact listening to what I was saying: my "social worker's speech," incongruously delivered in an atmosphere of armed police provocation. What I spoke of lay very close to the lives of these delegates, the right to homes and houses, the ending of hunger, the provision of medical care, the care of the aged, the sick, the young and the family.

Ironically, the next and last section of the charter was on peace and friendship. Peace and friendship, faced by guns, by armed police with searching hands, humiliating by their very presence. Yet the Congress of the People could not really be humiliated, could not be soiled. It rose triumphantly above this police action. It was no longer a draft but a reality; the program of the people, their own program for the future, their promise to their children of a land that should be free.

—Helen Joseph
from *Side by Side*

Ride Upon Death Chariot

They rode upon
the death chariot
to their Golgotha—three vagrants
whose papers to be in Caesar's empire
were not in order:

The sun
shrivelled their bodies
in the mobile tomb
as airtight as canned fish.

We're hot!
We're thirsty!
We're hungry!

The centurion
touched their tongues
with the tip
of a lance
dipped in apathy:

"Don't cry to me
but to Caesar who
crucifies you."

A woman came
to wipe their faces
She carried a dishcloth
full of bread and tea.
We're dying!

The centurion
washed his hands.

> —Oswald Mtshali
> from *To Whom It May Concern*

The Pension Jiveass

I lead her in,
A sepia figure 100 years old.
Blue ice chips gaze
And a red slash gapes:
"What does she want?"
I translate: "Pension, sir."
"Useless kaffir* crone,
Lazy as the black devil.
She'll get fuck-all."
I translate.

"My man toiled
and rendered himself impotent
With hard labor.
He paid tax like you.
I am old enough to get pension.

* Very derogatory way of referring to blacks, who strongly resent its use.

29

I was born before the great wars
And saw my father slit your likes' throats!"
I don't translate, but
She loses her pension anyhow.

—Mandlenkosi Langa
from *To Whom It May Concern*

I Am the Exile

I am the exile
am the wanderer
the troubadour
(whatever they say)

gentle I am, and calm
and with abstracted pace
absorbed in planning
courteous to servility

but wailings fill the chambers of my heart
and in my head
behind my quiet eyes
I hear the cries and sirens.

—Dennis Brutus
from *Poets to the People*

A visit to Chief Luthuli in banishment

We left Johannesburg at dawn on 1 May after the expiry of my ban at midnight. It was only when we were safely out on the open road heading north that I became really aware that I was free at last, free to go anywhere I chose, with whom I chose, no longer confined to Johannesburg or banned from gatherings. I was excited about our tour and the adventures to come, but underneath there was tremendous private joy. The bans were over and like the treason trial they faded into the past. I realized that they might be reimposed, especially in view of what I was doing in seeking out the banished people and their families, and I certainly intended to speak out about what I saw and heard when I returned. Somehow that did not matter as it was almost an occupational hazard and could not affect my present plans.

In Natal we met our beloved Chief Luthuli, President General of the African National Congress. He was restricted to the Groutville area, some miles from Stanger, where we had stayed overnight with Indian friends. Chief was banned from being with more than one person at a time, so we had to meet clandestinely by night, by special arrangement. We drove to Groutville through miles of sugarcane fields to stop on a curve of the road and wait for him.

Out of the darkness he came walking softly, and we heard him greet us. I could not see his face, but to hear his voice was enough and to sit beside him as we crowded him into our car, always watching the road for the lights of any other approaching vehicle. Time was precious because Chief had risked disastrous consequences to see us and to hear our reports on the banished people whom we had seen. If we were all caught together then Chief could be charged with attending a gathering.

I told him of the Matlala people, deep in Northern Transvaal, hundreds of miles from Johannesburg, where we had visited the wives of men who had been banished eight and ten years previously. The sun had been shining brightly as we drove around the rocky hills to meet these lonely women. They had put on their brightest headscarves and their gayest beads to welcome us but as, one by one, they told us their tragic stories, with Joe interpreting, the sky seemed less blue and the gay colors only served to deepen the lines of sorrow on the dark faces. Sometimes tears trickled slowly down their cheeks as they spoke to us. Only one man had returned.

—Helen Joseph
from *Side by Side*

Possibilities for a Man Hunted by SBs[*]

There's one of two possibilities
Either they find you or they don't
If they don't it's ok
But if they find you
There's one of two possibilities
Either they let you go or they banish you
If they let you go it's ok
But if they ban you
There's one of two possibilities

[*] SB - Special Branch of the police

Either you break your ban or you don't
If you don't it's ok
But if you break your ban
There's one of two possibilities
Either they find out or they don't
If they don't it's ok
But if they find out
There's one of two possibilities
Either they find you guilty or not guilty
If they find you not guilty it's ok
But if they find you guilty
There's one of two possibilities
Either they suspend your sentence or they jail you
If they suspend your sentence it's ok
But if they jail you
There's one of two possibilities
Either they release you
Or you fall from the tenth floor.

—Farouk Asvat
from *Voices from Within*

Crucifixion

Death

And so to kill a bug
they set a house on fire
to kill a fire
they flood a country
to save a country
drench the land in blood
to peg the frontiers of their color madness
they'll herd us into ghettoes
jail us
kill us slowly
because we are the Attribute
that haunts their dreams
because they are the blazing neon lights
they will not let us
be because we are the children of their Sin
they'll try to erase the evidence
because their deeds are howling from a fog
beyond their reach.

> . . . and we laughed and danced
> when news came of the death of that colossus
> —the death of a beast of prey.

What can we do with the ashes of a tyrant?
who will atone?
whose blood will pay for those of us who went
down under the tanks of fire?
And voices cried It's not enough,
a tyrant dead is not enough!
Vengeance is mine and yours and his,
says the testament of man
nailed to the boulder of pain.

> . . . and they say the butcher's mad
> who sank the knife into the tyrant's neck
> while the honorable men
> who rode his tanks of fire
> looked on
> as if they never heard that giants die

33

as they had lived,
and all about the frog who burst
when he pushed his energy
beyond the seams of his own belly.

What if I go as the unknown soldier
or attended by a buzzing fly?
what if my carcass were soaked in organ music,
or my ancestors had borne me home?
I hear already
echoes from a future time of voices
coming from a wounded bellowing multitude
cry Who will atone
Who will atone?

You want to know?
because I nourish
a deadly life within
my madness shall have blood.

> —Es'kia Mphalele
> from *Voices from Within*

Confession of Sins
A litany for leader and people

Woe to those who decree inequitous decrees, and the writers who keep writing oppression, to turn aside the needy from justice and to rob the poor of my people of their right. (Isaiah 10:1,2a)

> *Be gracious to us, O God, in your true love; in the fullness of your mercy blot out the misdeeds of Your people.*

Woe to the one who builds a house by unrighteousness, and upper rooms by injustice, who makes neighbors serve for nothing, and does not give them payment. (Jeremiah 22:13)

> *Be gracious to us, O God, in your true love; in the fullness of your mercy blot out the misdeeds of your people.*

O you who turn justice to wormwood, and cast down righteousness to the earth! . . . you who afflict the righteous, who take a bribe, and turn aside the needy in the gate. (Amos 5:7,12b)

> *Be gracious to us, O God in your true love; in the fullness of your mercy blot out the misdeeds of your people.*

Woe to those who are at ease in Zion. . . . who lie upon beds of ivory, and stretch themselves upon their couches. . . . who drink wine in bowls, and anoint themselves with the finest oils, but are not grieved over the ruin of Joseph! (Amos 6:1a, 4a,6)

Be gracious to us, O God in your true love; in the fullness of your mercy blot out the misdeeds of your people.

Shame on those who separate a husband from his wife, a mother from her children. This is the command of the Lord: "A man shall leave his father and mother and be joined to his wife, and the two shall become one. . . . What therefore God has joined together, let no person put asunder." (Matthew 19:5,6b)

Be gracious to us, O God in your true love; in the fullness of your mercy blot out the misdeeds of your people.

Jesus said, "The Spirit of the Lord is upon me, because he has anointed me to preach good news to the poor. He has sent me to proclaim release to the captives, and recovering of sight to the blind, to set at liberty those who are oppressed, to proclaim the acceptable year of the Lord." (Luke 4:18,19) ". . . I was hungry and you gave me no food, I was thirsty and you gave me no drink, I was a stranger and you did not welcome me, naked and you did not clothe me, sick and in prison and you did not visit me . . . Truly, I say to you, as you did it not to one of the least of these, you did it not to me." (Matthew 25:42,43,45)

Be gracious to us, O God in your true love; in the fullness of your mercy blot out the misdeeds of your people. AMEN.

The Sermon on the Mount

4. The Long Commitment to Nonviolent Change

It was in 1906 in South Africa that a young lawyer, Mahatma Gandhi, organized his first nonviolent protests against unjust laws. Gandhi, along with his followers, suffered violence and imprisonment for his actions. In 1912, the African National Congress (ANC) was founded with the same strong commitment to bring about change through peaceful means. The ANC maintained this commitment until 1961, the year after the Sharpeville massacre. In the years between 1912 and 1961 people began to lose faith that the white government would respond to peaceful marches and petitions, and the ANC began to include among its tactics demonstrations, boycotts and acts of civil disobedience. As the government responded to courageous criticism with ever more repressive measures, the risk of banning, imprisonment and exile grew. In the famous Treason Trial, which began in 1956, the government accused 156 people of participating in a conspiracy inspired by international communism to overthrow the South African state by violent means. The last of the accused were finally acquitted in 1961. (For more about South African movements for freedom and justice, see *South Africa's Moment of Truth*, especially Chapter Six).

Ritual

After the readings from this chapter, reflect on the following passages from Scripture:

Matthew 5:38-48. "Love your enemies and pray for those who persecute you."

Matthew 10:34-39. "Do not think that I have come to bring peace on earth. . ."

- In light of these texts, what do you think is expected of a Christian in a situation of violence like that in South Africa?

Consider the points along the spiral of violence as outlined by Brazilian Archbishop Dom Helder Camara:

> Stage One: The violence of exploitation and oppression
> Stage Two: The violent response of those who have been oppressed
> Stage Three: Violent repression of those who have rebelled, by those in power

- What do you think Christians need to do to break this spiral?
- Even within the context of armed struggle there remain people commited to nonviolence. How does this fact lend a purifying element to the struggle? Do you think it makes a difference in the quality of eventual peace?

Symbolic action: In a beautiful Hindu custom, one person carries a lighted candle around to each other person present. The light symbolizes God. One by one, each person reaches out his or her hands to the light. The hands are brought up before the face, there is a pause, and then the person moves her or his hands out to the side and down. It is as if we bathe our faces in the light, asking that our minds be purified in the light of God.

Close with a peace song, for example, "Let there be peace on earth."

Readings

Nonviolence

Nonviolence is "not a resignation from all real fighting against wickedness. . . . On the contrary, the nonviolence of my conception is a more active and real fight against wickedness than retaliation, whose very nature is to increase wickedness. I contemplate a mental and therefore moral opposition to immoralities. I seek entirely to blunt the edge of the tyrant's sword, not by putting up against it a sharper edged weapon, but by disappointing his expectation that I would be offering physical resistance. . . .

Nonviolence is an active force of the highest order. Consciousness of the living presence of God within one is undoubtedly the first requisite. . . .

If one has . . . pride, egoism, there is no nonviolence. Nonviolence is impossible without humility. . . .

Where there is love there is life. Hatred leads to destruction. Love is the strongest force the world possesses, and yet it is the humblest. I have no weapon but love to wield authority over anyone.

—Mahatma Gandhi
quoted in *The Message of Mahatma Gandhi*

Freedom via the Cross

These are the concluding paragraphs from Chief Albert Luthuli's statement after he was dismissed from his position as chief by the South African government in November 1952. Chief Luthuli, a deacon in the Congregational church at Groutville, Natal and a Nobel Peace Prize winner, was leader of the African National Congress when it was banned in 1961.

As for myself, with a full sense of responsibility and clear conviction, I decided to remain in the struggle for extending democratic rights and responsibilities to all sections of the South African community. I have embraced the Non-Violent Passive Resistance technique in fighting for freedom because I am convinced it is the only non-revolutionary, legitimate and human way that could be used by people denied, as we are, effective constitutional means to further aspirations. The wisdom or foolishness of this decision I place in the hands of the Almighty.

What the future has in store for me I do not know. It might be ridicule, imprisonment, concentration camp, flogging, banishment and even death. I only pray to the Almighty to strengthen my resolve so that none of these grim possibilities may deter me from striving, for the sake of the good name of our beloved country, South Africa, to make it a true democracy and a true union in form and spirit of all the communities of the land.

My only painful concern at times is that of the welfare of my family but I try even in this regard, in a spirit of trust and surrender to God's will as I see it, to say "God will provide."

It is inevitable that in working for Freedom some individuals and some families must take the lead and suffer: the Road to Freedom is via the Cross.

Mayibuye! Afrika!*

—Albert Luthuli
quoted in *Cry Justice*

---

* "Let Africa return!" or "Africa for the people!"

When Luthuli died in 1967, a young South African, Jennifer Davis, wrote these lines in tribute:

Bounded
You gave me knowledge
of freedom.

Silenced
You taught me how
to speak.

The Alexandra bus boycotts, 1943 and 1944

Just as our trial began in January, the great Alexandra Township bus boycott also began. Alexandra Township (popularly known as "Alex") was then a crowded black freehold township, some ten miles from the city. This boycott was not the first of its kind: that had been in 1943, when fifteen thousand Alex people walked ten miles to work and back again because they could not and would not accept an extra penny on the fares. I was then stationed as a WAAF* officer at the Union Grounds in Johannesburg, right on the road from Alex into the city. I saw the boycotters, washerwomen with their huge bundles of washing on their heads, the factory workers who worked a fifty-hour week, and old men and children too. Alex walked for nine days, through the sun and the wind and the rain—and the Alexandra people won. The busfares remained at four pence a journey, already more than ill-paid workers could afford.

A year later, Alex walked again. I saw it again, the determination that could conquer exhaustion, a people who could walk twenty miles a day for seven weeks. I marvelled at it, the passive resistance of a people who were denied any say about the conditions of life in which they worked and travelled. They lived in poverty, they worked for exploitative wages, they lived ten miles away from their jobs, because the whites would tolerate them no nearer. They travelled in grossly overcrowded buses, for which they stood for hours in queues and which already cost them eight pence a day. It was the extra two pence that brought them out in defiance. They would not pay it because their wages were too low to stand the extra shilling a week.

I realized more fully now that the bus boycott had a significance deeper that the refusal to pay the extra penny a ride. It was the

* Women's Auxiliary Air Force

only weapon available to the people of Alex, the weapon of sacrifice and determination, of undiminished fortitude, against which neither the bus company nor their allies, the police, could prevail.

—Helen Joseph
from *Side by Side*

The task of reconciliation

Dr. Beyers Naudé is one of the most prophetic Christian leaders in South Africa. On accepting the Niebuhr Award at the University of Chicago in 1974, Beyers Naudé focused on the issue of nonviolent change:

This is one of the crucial questions with which the Christian Church and the Christian community throughout the world is faced, together with all the inhabitants of the globe. Deep differences of conviction are being held and expressed on this issue not only within but also outside the organized Church. I do not think that Christ gives us the right to judge or condemn those who, in finding themselves in such situations of tyranny and oppression, have come to the conclusion that, having tried all else, there is no option left to procure liberation but through violence. But I hold the conviction that this is not, cannot be, and will never be the truly satisfying answer which God has made available to his children on earth.

We are committed, in accordance with our understanding of the Christian faith, to do everything in our power to achieve these goals by peaceful means; we are committed to the task of reconciliation based on justice and of Christian liberation through justice without which no lasting reconciliation could be procured.

—Beyers Naudé
quoted in *Naudé: Prophet to South Africa*

Nelson Mandela at the Treason Trial

I was born in Umtata, Transkei, on 18 July 1918. My father, Chief Henry, was a polygamist with four wives. Neither he nor my mother ever went to school. My father died in 1930, after which David Dalindyebo, the acting Paramount Chief of the tribe, became my guardian.

I am related to both Sabata Dalindyebo, the present Paramount Chief of Tembuland, and to Kaizer Matanzima, Chief Minister for the Transkei. Both are, according to Tembu customs, my nephews.

I hold the degree of Bachelor of Arts from the University of South

Africa, and am a qualified solicitor. I married Winnie, daughter of Columbus Madikizela, the present Minister of Agriculture in the Transkei, in 1958, while an accused in the Treason Trial. I have five children, three by a former marriage and two with Winnie.

My political interest was first aroused when I listened to elders of our tribe in my village as a youth. They spoke of the good old days before the arrival of the White man. Our people lived peacefully under the democratic rule of their kings and counsellors and moved freely all over their country. Then the country was ours. We occupied the land, the forests and the rivers. We set up and operated our own government; we controlled our own armies, and organized our own trade and commerce.

The elders would tell us about the liberation and how it was fought by our ancestors in defense of our country, as well as the acts of valor performed by generals and soldiers during those epic days. I hoped, and vowed then, that among the pleasures that life might offer me, would be the opportunity to serve my people and make my own humble contribution to their struggle for freedom.

—Nelson Mandela
from *The Struggle is My Life*

Reprinted by permission of Pathfinder Press. Copyright © 1986 by the International Defence and Aid Fund and Pathfinder Press.

Mandela's testimony, 1960

The following is extracted from the testimony by Mandela, responding as speaker for the accused to questions from the bench, the prosecution and the defense lawyers on the content of African National Congress documents and the question of violent intent on the part of those on trial.

Prosecution: Do you think that your People's Democracy could be achieved by a process of gradual reforms? Suppose, as a result of pressure, the ruling class were to agree next month to a qualified franchise for the Africans, an educational test perhaps—not a stringent one—and next year, as a result of further pressure, a more important concession is made—a further concession is made in 1962, and so on over a period of ten or twenty years—do you think that People's Democracy could be achieved in that fashion?

Mandela: Well, this is how I approach the question. I must explain at the outset that the Congress, as far as I know, has never sat down to discuss the question. . . . We demand universal adult franchise and we are prepared to exert economic pressure to attain our demands, and we will launch defiance campaigns, stay-at-homes, either singly or together, until the Government should say, "Gentlemen, we cannot have this state of affairs, laws are being defied, and this whole situation created by stay-at-homes. Let's talk." In my own view I would say, Yes, let us talk, and the Government would say, "We think the Europeans at present are not ready for a type of government where there might be a domination by non-Europeans. We think we should give you sixty seats. The African population to elect sixty Africans to represent them in Parliament. We will leave the matter over for five years and we will review it at the end of five years."

In my view, that would be a victory, my lords; we would have taken a significant step towards the attainment of universal adult suffrage for Africans, and we would then for the five years say, we will suspend civil disobedience; we won't have any stay-at-homes, and we will then devote the intervening period for the purpose of educating the country, the Europeans, to see that these changes can be brought about and that it would bring about better racial understanding, better racial harmony in the country. I'd say we should accept it, but, of course, I would not abandon the demands for the extension of universal franchise to all Africans. That's how I see it, my lords. Then at the end of the five-year period we will have discussions and if the Government says, "We will give you again forty more seats," I might say that that is quite sufficient. Let's accept it, and still demand that the franchise should be extended, but for the agreed period we should suspend civil disobedience, no stay-at-homes. In that way we would eventually be able to get everything that we want; we shall have our People's Democracy, my lords. That is the view I hold—whether that is Congress' view I don't know, but that is my view.

* * *

Bench: Mandela, assuming you were wrong in your beliefs, do you visualize any future action on behalf of the Government, by the Government? Because I think the evidence suggests that you could not expect the Government to soften in its views. Have you any future plans in that event?

Mandela: No, my lord. I don't think that the Congress has ever believed that its policy of pressure would ultimately fail. The Congress, of course, does not expect that one single push to coerce the Government to change its policy will succeed; the Congress expects that over a period, as a result of a repetition of these pressures, together with world opinion, that the Government, notwithstanding its attitude of ruling Africans with an iron hand, that notwithstanding that, the methods which we are using will bring about a realization of our aspirations.

Prosecution: Mr. Mandela, whether or not these would be successful ultimately, one thing is clear, is it not, and this is that the African National Congress held the view, and propagated the view, that in resisting pressure by the Congress Movement, the ruling class—the Government—would not hesitate to retaliate—would not hesitate to use violence and armed force against the Congress Movement?

Mandela: Yes, the Congress was of that view, my lords. We did expect force to be used, as far as the Government is concerned, but as far as we are concerned, we took the precautions to ensure that violence will not come from our side.

Bench: What were those precautions?

Mandela: Well, my lord, for example in 1952 when we launched the Defiance Campaign, and secondly, my lord, you will notice that we frequently use "stay-at-home," not "strike" in the ordinary sense. Now, my lord, in a strike what is usually done is to withdraw workers from a particular industry and then have pickets to prevent the people from working in those industries which are boycotted. But the Congress theory was that to have pickets might attract police violence. We deliberately decided to use "stay-at-home" where people are asked to remain in their houses.

Prosecution: As far as you know, has the onward march of the liberatory movement continued to manifest itself?

Mandela: Yes it has. Congress has become much more powerful and much more strong today.

Prosecution: And in your opinion is the possibility of this violence to which you refer therefore heightened—increased?

Mandela: Oh, yes; we felt that the Government will not hesitate to massacre hundreds of Africans in order to intimidate them not to oppose its reactionary policy.

* * *

Bench: I want to know whether the Congress Alliance discussed or considered whether the—whether White supremacy in South Africa would without a show of arms surrender that which if surrendered would mean its end?

Mandela: No, my lord. The Congress has considered the question from the point of view firstly of its experience. The Whites being eager to retain political power exclusively for themselves—

Bench: That was considered?

Mandela: That was considered. It was also considered that through this policy of exerting pressure we will force the Whites by using our numbers, our numerical preponderance, in forcing them to grant us what we demand, even against their will. We considered that, and we felt that that was possible.

Bench: How would you use your numerical numbers to force White supremacy to give what you want?

Mandela: For example by staying at home and not going to work, using our economic power for the purpose of attaining our demands. Now, my lord, we were not looking—we were not hoping that these demands were going to be realized during the period of the indictment, no. We had in mind that in the forseeable future it will be possible for us to achieve these demands, and we worked on the basis that Europeans themselves in spite to the wall of prejudice and hostility which we encountered, that they can never remain indifferent indefinitely to our demands, because we are hitting them in the stomach with our policy of economic pressure. It is a method which is well organized. The Europeans dare not look at it with indifference. They would have to respond to it and indeed, my lord, they are responding to it.

—Nelson Mandela
from *The Struggle Is My Life*

Memories Don't Break Chains

Days go by like everyday.
We bury the dead who died
cruel and strange deaths.
Yet as we said
memory is like water
Yet that is not enough
memories don't break chains
nor does dying like dogs or cattle

or throwing stones and bricks at mad armed men
nor do lies at the U.N. or anywhere else.
My people, tell me
what does, what breaks chains?

We need the truth
we need to hear words
and if lips tremble
they should tremble only because they know

Too much blood has been spilled
Please my countrymen, can someone say a word of wisdom
It is too late
Blood, no matter how little of it
when it spills on the brain—
on the memory of a nation
it is as if the sea floods the earth
The lights go out
mad hounds howl in the dark
Ah, we've become familiar with horror
the heart of our country
when it makes its pulse
ticking time
wounds us
My countrymen, can someone who understands
    that it is now too late
who knows that exploitation and oppression
    are brains which being
insane only know violence
can someone teach us how to mount the wound and fight.

The bright eye of the night keeps whispering and whispering
the shadows form and unfold
the trees hide in the dark
the grass whistles
the night is silent with experience
this night
in these parts of the world.

—Mongane Serote
from *The Night Keeps Winking*

5. Black Consciousness: New Hope

The struggle for freedom and justice in South Africa has been a long one. Over the years each generation's frustration would build up until people would make a concerted effort to effect change. And each time this effort would be so ruthlessly repressed that another decade would pass before the black community and white liberals could recover their strength and begin the next major effort. Throughout the years, resistance continued, and in the late 1960s a new phenomenon developed: the black consciousness movement. Influenced initially by the U.S. movement of the same name, black consciousness was introduced into South Africa through the University Christian Movement, of which Steve Biko was a leader. The aim of black consciousness was to break through the effects of cultural domination that had robbed blacks of confidence in their own identity. In the end, it brought about a qualitative change in the lives of black people in South Africa—a new belief in themselves that was like a veld fire that could not be stopped. Biko's own life and his death in detention gave birth to the courage that lay behind the 1976 Soweto uprising, the 1980 school boycotts in the Cape, and the surge of grassroots democracy that arose throughout South Africa in the early 1980s. As Jesus said, "Unless a grain of wheat falls into the earth and dies, it remains alone; but if it dies, it bears much fruit." (John 12:24)

Ritual

The twentieth century is an age of martyrs similar to that experienced by the early church under the Roman Empire. Think of some of the martyrs you know about from Central America, Chile, the Philippines and the civil rights movement in the United States.

Symbolic Action: Prepare a tray of earth. After the readings, read aloud the text, "Unless a grain of wheat falls into the earth and dies, it remains alone, but if it dies, it bears much fruit."

Continue by reading the following aloud: We feel tremendous sadness at the death of Steve Biko and the deaths of all who have died violently in detention and exile, among them, Ahmed Timol, Abraham Tiro, Ruth First; at the deaths of the many young people killed in the 1976 uprisings and afterwards; for those executed because of their involvement in armed struggle, people like Solomon Mahlangu, whose last message before death was, "Tell my people that I love them." Jesus said, "Greater love has no one than this, that one lay down one's life for a friend" (John 15:13). As Christians we try to hold on to our belief that life does come through death. The whole of nature gives us testimony that this is true. So even as we read the daily newspapers and struggle against despair, even as we mourn for those who have been killed, let us plant and water these seeds, grains of wheat, renewing our faith that these dying seeds will bring forth much fruit.

Make furrows in the soil and ask each person to come forward and place a seed in a furrow. The last two people cover the seeds with earth and water them. Ask someone to take care of the seeds, watering them and putting them in the sun, and to bring them back to the group for the last session.

Close with the poem "Living Is Forever."

Readings

Memories of Steve

Many have died in detention and they are all remembered. In some cases the memories are vivid only within family circles. In other cases their lives still radiate light throughout the black community. Steve Biko was one of these.

Steve was my second son's peer, colleague and confidant. To this day I have dear, yet sad memories of a familiar threesome: Steve Biko, Barney Pityana and Justice Moloto, the last my son. They would walk into the house without announcing where they came from or where they were bound for. "Good morning," or "Evening, Mom;" "We know you are fine. We need a good meal, Mom—is it possible? . . ."

What mother could refuse three charming young men such a dear request? On the contrary, I often felt privileged to do anything for them. At the end of their meal they would leave as casually as they had arrived.

I have shared a platform with this son of Africa at a number of SASO [South African Students Organization] workshops when an aspect of black consciousness was under review. Then, I saw another side of Steve. I saw in him a clear-thinking researcher, a hardliner in language, and in action a planner, and above all a leader and soldier of great courage. Sometimes I felt that he and his colleagues put black consciousness before idealism, but at the end of the workshop, without any effort or discussion, we assumed our roles of adult and youth, of mother and son or daughter.

Steve's involvement, commitment and charisma had earned him international recognition when he met his untimely death. And it is true to say of him that within this country, most especially among his own people, Steve was a model of black consciousness— a concept which has created awareness among blacks about who they are and were, and helped to build up the determination to regain their strength and personality as a nation—for young and old alike. He was respected, loved and highly valued and will always be remembered for his outstanding leadership. He told his mother, when trying to help her understand his commitment, "I have a special mission to work with my people."

. . . Yes, Steve Biko is dead; but his spirit will live forever.

—Ellen Kuzwayo
from *Call Me Woman*

A definition of black consciousness

Black consciousness is the realization by the blacks of the need to rally together with their brothers and sisters around the cause of their oppression—the blackness of their skin—and to operate as a group in order to rid themselves of the shackles that bind them to perpetual servitude. It shows new realization that by seeking to run away from themselves and to emulate the white race blacks are insulting the intelligence of whoever created them black. Black consciousness, therefore, takes cognizance of the deliberateness of God's plan in creating black people black. It seeks to infuse the black community with a new-found pride in themselves, their efforts, their value systems, their culture, their religion and their outlook to life.

1. Being black is not a matter of pigmentation—being black is a reflection of a mental attitude.

2. Merely by describing yourself as black you have started on a road towards emancipation, you have committed yourself to fight against all forces that seek to use your blackness as a stamp that

48

marks you out as a subservient being.

—Steve Biko
from *I Write What I Like*

Masechaba

Africa
mother of children
impatient
reluctant
to be like the rivers that
meander to the seas

Africa
mother of children
destitute
dying but
determined
to prescribe themselves freedom
to describe themselves free

Africa
your children no longer nestle in your arms
crawl on your belly
accept their fate (dumb, silent)
your children have rejected their garments
of indifference
of docile acceptance
your children no longer (your children) sleep and do not sleep

Africa
the voice of your children
erodes the mist-shrouded mountains
like hungry rain
and cuts through the valleys
like the pounding rivers
that ravage and rape your fields

Africa
today your rivers heal our wounds

your fields offer us refuge
and your mountains do not silence,
no they hold and harbor
the sounds of warriors
answering the call for justice.

—Ilva Mackay
from *Malibongwe*

White Lies

Humming Maggie.
Hit by a virus,
the Caucasian Craze,
sees horror in the mirror.
Frantic and dutifully
she corrodes a sooty face,
braves a hot iron comb
on a scrubby scalp.
I look on.

I know pure white,
a white heart,
white, peace, ultimate virtue.
Angels are white
angels are good.
Me I'm black,
black as sin stuffed in a snuff-tin.
Lord, I've been brainwhitewashed.

But for Heaven's sake God,
just let me be.
Under cover of my darkness
let me crusade.
On a canvas stretching from here
to Dallas, Memphis, Belsen, Golgotha,
I'll daub a white devil.
Let me teach black truth.
That dark clouds aren't a sign of doom,
but hope. Rain. Life.

Let me unleash a volty bolt of black,
so all around may know black right.

—Stanley Motjuwadi
from *Voices from Within*

Childhood in Soweto

There are no playgrounds
no parks
but plenty dust
children compete
cars, bicycles, hungry mongrels
narrow streets and garbage
there is no childhood
in Soweto

There are no stars
to twinkle twinkle little eyes
no rockets
launch dreams
no new years resolutions rise
through the thick
blanket of smoke
in Soweto
dust aplenty

There is no poverty
of sirens
sprinters' footsteps
coattail-ends whisk away
jack-boot doors howl
men women children terrorized
huddle in raids
bundled in rage
passes passes passes
there is no childhood
no adulthood
in Soweto

only plenty
dust

But I have seen new plays
in one act
announcing the birth
of childhood
grenades clearing the night
of blinders of smoke
and hurdles
passing the child
into star-grappling teens
adulthood without passes
in Soweto

in towns and cities
north and east
growing from
Soweto

—Lerato Kumalo
from *Malibongwe*

Ideologies

Manifesto

This then is our choice and task
Change is going to come

Before the inevitable choice for life
There is only solitude and hungerpang
A lake of pain whose impartial waters
Heave and trace an inexorable path straight
Through centuries dazed by mazes of colonial ties

> Were you there when
> They killed your heroes
> Where were you when
> They killed Lumumba
> And later sold our land
> To vampires from Bonn
> Were you there when
> They killed Lutuli, Malcolm,
> And the Communist Councilman from Harlem

Yes Mandela we shall be moved and move
We are Man enough to immortalize your song
We are Man enough to root out the predators
Who traded in the human spirit
For black cargoes and material superprofits
We emerge to sing a song of Fire and Love

We emerge to prove again life cannot be enslaved
In chains or imprisoned in an island inferno
We emerge to stand life on her multiple feet
Across the face of the earth

And let no choleric charlatan tell you
It will be by chance
Our voice in unison with our poet's proudly says

Change is going to come

—Keorapetse Kgositsile
from *Poets to the People*

The Chain Must Be Broken . . .

This section of the longer poem, "A Chain Must Be Broken," is about Steve Biko.

Reader 1	I walk the night of this land
	I hear crickets chirp
	and the stars keep whistling and whistling.
	Listen—
	these (fucking) stars
	whistled like this
	when one man
	walked like all of us
	then he was naked
	then chained on his leg
	then on the floor
	covered with a blanket
	in a land-rover
	1,000 km in that state—
	to another cell
	where he woke up one morning
	naked
	chained
	alone
	with a brain damage, his blankets wet
	his eyes staring
	I dare say
	his damaged memory told him he was going to die
	in a cell
	chained on the leg
	wet and naked, alone,
	the 45th
	to be in the hands of mad men who believed in God
Reader 2	Yet these men did not know
	what this man knew
	that he would make it for his funeral
	that the people would claim his battered remains
	that he would not be counted among the countless
	many

stolen
from their homes—
streets
fields
hut
to disappear as if never born
except that they now float like rotting corpses on
water
on the memory of the people
Steve knew this
he had to, he was a bright boy.
So there was a funeral in Kingwilliamstown

Reader 3   There have been may funerals in my country
funerals
of bright babies
whose blood was spilled in the streets
by fire-power of oppression
there are commemorations world wide
for my countrymen
some of whom fought and lost
some fell defenseless
We in my country fought and fell and keep fighting
ask Blood River*
and Soweto will answer:

each line a   School children took to the streets one day.
different   There will never be another Soweto.
voice   There are many kinds of deaths, and Soweto knows
            them all;
South Africa too, and Southern Africa.
You cannot kill children like cattle and then hope that
            guns are a monopoly.

women's   We made love in strange places in ghettoes. We gave
voices   birth in these holes. We learned from pain and sorrow
of having lost our children to so many and such cruel
deaths as malnutrition or murder or madness, dying

* The battle fought December 16, 1838 between Boers and Zulus. Several thousand Zulu warriors were slaughtered as they fought against guns with spears.

	while throwing spears or stones and being shot dead.
Reader 4	We must now claim our land, even if we die in the process.
	Our history is a culture of resistance.
different voices	Ask Mozambique
	—Angola
	—Zimbabwe
	—Namibia
All	Ask South Africa
	Yes—
	from Blood River
	to Sharpeville to Soweto
	we know now
	that oppression has at last been unmasked
Reader 2	we ask, why oppress us
Reader 1	to exploit us
Reader 2	why exploit us
All	now we know—
	that the chain must be broken

—Mongane Wally Serote
from *The Night Keeps Winking*

Living Is Forever

Sprouting
Rising
Living
Dying
Sprouting
Rising
Living! Living! Living!

When they put us in jail, Brother Neto*
They aim to kill us
But dying, we sprout anew

* A leader of the freedom struggle in Angola

Sprouting
Rising
Living! Living! Living!

Young shoots break the soil's surface
Like head, neck, shoulders, arms
Legs, toes, fingers all stretched in heliotropic longing

Sprouting
Rising
Living! Living! Living!

O, Brother Neto! You and Africa are one
You and Africa were one in the year of Creation
It was spring, then summer, then autumn
Then winter, then spring, then autumn

Sprouting
Rising
Living! Living! Living!

Now the fruits hang in rich clusters
Aromatic juices flow between the fingers
Moisten parched throats
And hands dipped in the earth's cornucopia
Tantalize the nostrils as they pass to the mouth
watering copiously

Rising
Living! Living! Living!

And the seeds dropped in the soil
Are quickened to life again
By the sun, the rain and the wind

Dying
Rising! Rising! Rising!

For the sun's crucifixion on the western horizon
Is a prelude to its radiant resurrection in the eastern skies
ARISE AND LIVE!

—Daniel P. Kunene
from *A Seed Must Seem to Die*

6. Women Tell Their Stories

After years of silence, African women have started to tell their stories. Their personalities come across strong and clear in the readings that follow, as do their immense and intensely personal anxieties. For in addition to the constant struggle against poverty and the tension that accompanies the forced separation of families, mothers now face a new fear: where are their children when they disappear? Have they been detained or shot? Are they in hiding or staying with friends? Or have they gone into exile?

Ritual

Arrange in advance for an exhibition of photographs showing the faces of ordinary South African women in everyday life. (The photo set available from the International Defense and Aid Fund is excellent; see Resources.) Before the readings, invite the group to walk around the room looking at the faces in the photographs, then to choose one face and stand in silence before it, trying to imagine what it would be like to live that woman's life.

Scripture: Jesus' mother experienced the kind of suffering that many women go through in situations of poverty and oppression in South Africa and other parts of the world. Consider Mary as she is described in the following passages:

Matthew 2:13-15. As a refugee mother.
Mark 3:20,21 and 31-35. As a mother confused at her son's political activity and wondering if he is mad.
John 18, 19. As the mother of a child who disappears, is detained, tortured and put to death.
Consider also the women who see Jesus on his way to Calvary (Luke 23:27-31).

Symbolic action: Sharing the food of the poor.

Traditionally, women in most countries grow, cook and serve the food their families eat. Day after day, month after month, year after year, the words of Jesus, "I was hungry and you gave me food," apply to them. As we honor the millions of unknown but heroic women in South Africa who struggle to keep family life going against overwhelming pressures, the most fitting symbol is to prepare the simplest meal. As Gandhi said: "There are many people so poor that God cannot appear to them in any form except bread." This certainly gives us a new sense of the meaning of the Lord's Supper.

In many parts of Africa, the traditional food is cornmeal cooked with salt and water. *Sadza*, in Zimbabwe, has the consistency of mashed potatoes; *posho* in South Africa is much harder. It is eaten with a sauce, very rarely with meat; the poor are lucky if they can make it with wild greens, pumpkin leaves or kale.

Two dishes, one of *posho* and one of boiled greens, can be prepared before the readings start. To make *posho*, boil water with a little salt; add cornmeal, stirring continually until the mixture is the consistency of hard mashed potatoes. Keep the dishes warm and then place them on a table set simply with items from Africa.

Before the meal, the hostess goes to each person present with a jug of water and a basin. In a symbolic cleansing before the ritual meal she pours the water over their hands into the basin and offers them a towel. For the meal, each person comes up to the table, rolls a little *posho* into a ball with the fingers, dips it into the bowl of greens and eats it. The basin of water should be ready so that everyone can wash their hands again afterwards. South African music in the background would be appropriate for this ritual. Close with a spontaneous litany for the women of South Africa and other women who have to struggle for their own and their children's survival.

Readings

Motherhood

The women of our village
Like a travelling herd of giraffes
Their heads thrust against the blue afternoon
On the ridge of the earth they walk like shadows.

Their songs echo into the darkness of the evening
With all creatures and all the whispering winds

They stretch their arms and their fingers and their long harvests
They are the women of plenty who gave to the earth.

Suddenly the sky wears the milky way
And the fertile horizon swells
And the shadow lies down like a little hill
The moon accompanies the birth of our children.

All these maternal powers surround the earth
And our women are no longer singing
Their round bellies heave with pounding sighs
And all that lies dormant breaks through the giant shell.

They have returned to the high stone,
From underneath the feet of the morning
Young creatures begin to inhabit the earth
This is their home, the everlasting cycle.

—Mazisi Kunene
from *The Ancestors and the Sacred Mountain*

Making pots

Pottery was a woman's skill. Many mothers over the years have
been engaged in this craft. They chose the clay for the pots (big
and small) with great care and made and maintained the condition
and quality of the tools they used for shaping and cutting their
products. It fascinated me to watch them work on a clay pot from
start to finish. The selection and working on the clay to be used
seemed tedious to the onlookers; but to the one who made the
pot it seemed a great joy. They sifted the clay carefully, and mixed
and worked on it at length, testing it and remixing it if necessary.

Their skill was well displayed when they rolled the clay between
their hands, taking care to put sufficient pressure on the clay to
avoid it being uneven. They handled it with great dexterity,
rendering the rolls supple, flexible, and ready to take the shape
and size of the planned pot. The coils of clay were piled every
one on top of the other in a long continuous roll, working from
the base upward. Then followed the swift, light fingerwork—gently
smoothing the clay into one even, solid creation, so taking the shape
of the finished pot. At this stage, tools—such as a piece of sharp
zinc—were used to level the edges of the mouth of the pot. The
finished product was carefully protected from the weather with
a light covering and left to dry—a long, delicate process. The women

would carefully examine their pots for possible cracks. In the absence
of these, the pots were prepared for firing and, finally, for cooling.
It was a very involved process which produced clay pots of different
shapes and sizes, for varied purposes, some as household utensils,
others as ornaments. The finished product was of high quality.

Marketing the pots was not a problem, as they were made to
order for neighbors. The sales were on the barter system. There
was no problem of delivery.

—Ellen Kuzwayo
from *Call Me Woman*

The African Pot

it is round and fat and squat
it has no handle and the rim has no spout
at first it seems as if the colors have
no coordination and no rhythm
the yellow and brown stripes circle
the pot in quick diagonals

i puzzle over the absence of the handle
and then suddenly i think of a young woman
wearing beads walking to a river with
the pot gracefully balanced on her head

and then the colors begin to rhyme
yellow zigzagging around the top
makes me think of harvest time of golden corn
of dancers around an autumn fire of ripe fruit
and of men drinking homebrewed beer

and as i stroke the brown
i can almost feel the full earth between
my fingers earth that echoes the thunderous
stamp of warriors going to war earth that
offers base accompaniment to dancing feet
i can almost see an ox pulling a plough
steered by man of infinite patience
making ordered rows of upturned loam

the maker made this pot
with a song in his heart

and a vision in his eyes
lifting it up i can almost hear
him say

i am man
life is but clay in my hands
creation is at my finger
—Fhazel Johennesse
from *The Oak and the Peach*

Black Mother

(To all suffering of our country, South Africa)

I have looked at your ash grey face
At your dry chapped muttering mouth and expressionless eyes
Muttering about rent increases and rising g.s.t.*
On a chilly Monday morning

Suffering mother, on Sunday you buried your husband
Killed by lung cancer in a mine hospital
Today you are rushing to George Grey Avenue
To cheer up Pieter and Johanna
Who did not get to tour Europe in their father's jet

Black Mother, you work and laugh during the day
You pray, cry and hope at night
Daylight hides our thoughts and feelings
Darkness is the time for aspirations
Black Mother, FEAR is the ruler

—Wonga Tabata
from *Staffrider*

The experience of black nannies when they grow old

Through my involvement with voluntary welfare work, I have met many old women (former domestic workers). Some of them have been sent by their employers to the notorious "transit camps" in

* general sales tax

Soweto. Some employers had made promises to maintain them but never come back to honor such undertakings. The "transit camps" are set aside by the West Rand Administration Board for destitute black people in the district of Johannesburg, theoretically as staging posts, on their way to "resettlement" in a black "homeland."

I have listened to heartbreaking stories from some of the inmates there, old men and women, who live under appallingly congested conditions. Most of them receive a negligible amount from a pension fund; and some depend on pitiable savings to provide them with day-to-day supplies. Their salaries, which should have been such as to make it possible to save for rainy days, were so low that they literally lived from hand to mouth. These old people had served their employers with loyalty and showed great love for their employer's children. In return, they were dismissed from their work and discarded to transit camps to be forgotten and to wait for their deaths with regrets and great bitterness.

These great mothers of South Africa brought up and nurtured children of all communities, sometimes at the sacrifice of their own children. I quote one such mother: "Struth God,* the children I brought up, some of them are doctors today, yes, but not one of them thinks of me today." Indeed, thousands of black mothers could echo the same statement.

—Ellen Kuzwayo
from *Call Me Woman*

The sharp end of the knife

Let's forget for a minute that we are women. Let's say we are the mothers. We are mothers—see what is taking place in this country. A mother will hold the knife on the sharp end. Today we see our people being sent to jail every day—there's detentions, the courts are crowded every day, people in exile, people rotting in jails.

Now we, as mothers, what must we say? We say to you—we are sick and tired of what is happening. We see our children being sent to jail for nothing. We see people being sent to the borders— they are going to kill people. As mothers we endorse what others have been saying. A national convention must be called so that our leaders must come and solve the problem which is confronting our country. We've got people in exile—we tell the government we want those leaders to come home. We have got people who are rotting in jails—we say we want those people to come home.

—Ma Frances Baard
from *Vukani Makhosikazi*†

* "God's truth", or "as true as God" (colloquial)
† The title of this book is Zulu for "Rise up, women"

Shopping

Last week I went to the shop and I bought food. A woman in front of me was also buying food. She was old. She had the food in the basket and she was unpacking it. But when the time came to pay, she didn't have enough money. So she struggled to decide "what can I take out . . . I can't do without this, I can't do without this, I can't do without that . . . what must I take out. I need everything that is in the basket." She had to take out one of the important things she needed to feed her children. Because she could not afford it.

It is always asked, "Why do people steal so much?" Because your stomach doesn't understand "there is not money" . . . your stomach screams when it wants.

This tax that we are paying goes to pay the huge salaries of government officials who oppress us, and for the ammo that kills our children. That's what we are paying for.

How long are we going to tolerate this oppression? Some people say the release will cost us much. But where does release lie? It lies with us working people.

—Liz Abrahams
from *Vukani Makhosikazi*

Knocks on the Door

The children have gone
From the breasts of their beloved mothers
They have left at dawn
Oh! black mothers, in tears.
When they come back
With anger, fire and spears
They will knock harder on this bolted door
Oh! I fear and hate violence
Do you hear me in the three chambers?

—Wonga Tabata
from *Staffrider*

Do Not Ask Me

Do not ask me, mother, if they're gone
I fear to tell you
they left me in the middle of the night
turned their backs on the warmth of the hearth
and for the last time
heard the home rooster crowing
Do not ask me, mother, where they went
Tracks on watery dew-bells
as puny feet brushed the morning grass
have evaporated in the heat of the sun's kindness
and the hunting bloody-snouted hounds
have lost the trail

But to you I will whisper:
Look where the willows weep
The willows of the Mohokare River
have seen the forbidden sight
tiny feet in a mad choreographer's dance
from shore to shore
wading on the sandy bed
And the waters washed and levelled up the sands
Nor will the willows point their dropping limbs
to say where they've gone

Do not ask me, mother, why they left
Need I tell you

They took the aamasi bird* out of the forbidden pot
and bade it fill their clay bowls to the very brim
they'd been so hungry
so long

Then an army with giant boots
came towering over them
Brand new guns

* A symbol of knowledge

65

made to silence little children who cry
glinting in the African sun
The gun-toters threw the aamasi bird
back into the pot
and wrote on it with the government's ink
FOR WHITE CHILDREN ONLY
and henceforth it was guarded day and night
by one hundred bayoneted soldiers
And the children raised their fists
and shouted:
Aamasi! Aamasi! We demand the aamasi bird!
Amandla! Amandla! Ngawethu!*

Now they've been gathered up
in the wings of the Giant Bird
to the place of the circumcision
far, far away

And the village waits
for the day of their return
to conquer

> —Daniel P. Kunene
> from *A Seed Must Seem to Die*

An inspiration

A young and active woman in the struggle has this to say abut
our aged leaders: "I'll never forget the day, the 4th April 1918. I
was very new to the struggle and a friend invited me to the United
Women's Organization launch. The chair asked for discussion from
the floor . . . no one spoke . . . then a frail old woman in a wheelchair
started speaking. Everyone was suddenly quiet while this woman
spoke these powerful words:

You who have no work, speak.
You who have no homes, speak.
You who have no schools, speak.
You who have to run like chickens from the vulture, speak.

---

* "Power is Ours" or "Power to the People!" A slogan used frequently at demonstrations,
rallies and other public anti-apartheid gatherings in South Africa.

Let us share our problems so that we can solve them together.
We must free ourselves.
Men and women must share housework.
Men and women must work together in the home and out in the
    world.
There are no creches and nursery schools for our children.
There are no homes for the aged.
Women must unite to fight for these rights.
I opened the road for you,
you must go forward.

—Mama Dora Tamana
from *South Africa: A Different Kind of War*

Here I Stand

Here I stand
With no child in sight
Did I conceive to throw away?

My children have gone to the towns
To seek bread
They never returned
They went to the mines
To dig gold
They died in shaft 14
They went to the mills
They died in the grinding stones
They went to ISCOR*
Their hands were guillotined
My children
Children of blood, blood of my children

—Boitumelo
from *Voices of Women*

* Iron and Steel Corporation, owned by the South African government

7. Four Great South African Women

August 9 is celebrated as "Women's Day" in South Africa in commemoration of the great demonstration held on that day in 1956, when twenty thousand women each handed a letter to the prime minister in Pretoria. The letters protested the proposed law that black women would at any time be subject to instant arrest if they were not carrying "passes." This was part of the government's policy of "influx control," preventing women in the countryside from joining their husbands who had gone to work in towns. Lilian Ngoyi and Helen Joseph, two of the women featured in this chapter, were among the main organizers of this historic protest.

Lilian Ngoyi was the leader of the African women's resistance movement in the 1950s. She was a woman of immense courage and initiative, with great charm and a wonderful sense of humor. Realizing the devastating effect that enforcing the pass law would have on family life and children, she travelled across South Africa persuading women to join the protest. Ngoyi was a member of the African National Congress and a founding member of the South African Federation of Women, a unique multiracial movement committed to women's rights. Her enthusiasm and commitment inspired women to engage in political action that went far beyond the traditional women's role. The government was well aware of Lilian Ngoyi's influence, and she was one of the 156 people accused in the famous Treason Trial of 1956-60. Following the trial she was banned for many years. At her death in 1980 she was mourned throughout the country.

Helen Joseph, an English social worker, arrived in South Africa in 1930. She and Lilian Ngoyi became close friends as they organized the 1956 demonstration and went through the Treason Trial together, but years of banning and house arrest prevented them from seeing one another for eleven years. Now in her eighties, Helen

Joseph is probably more loved and respected by blacks than any other white woman in South Africa. She has also been very close to the Mandela family. Her recently published autobiography is titled *Side by Side.*

Ellen Kuzwayo also recently published her autobiography, *Call Me Woman.* The title reminds us that many white South Africans refer to their domestic workers as "girls," even when they are grandmothers—a deeply-resented insult. In her preface to *Call Me Woman,* Nadine Gordimer, the South African novelist, writes:

> Ellen Kuzwayo's life has been lived as a black woman in South Africa, with all this implies. But it is also the life of that generation of women anywhere—in different epochs and different countries—who have moved from the traditional place in home and family system to an industrialized world in which they had to fight to make a place for themselves. Perhaps the most striking aspect of this book is the least obvious. It is an intimate account of the psychological road from the old, stable, nineteenth-century African equivalent of a country squire's home to the black proletarian dormitories of Johannesburg. Living through this, Ellen Kuzwayo emerges not only as a brave and life-affirming person; she represents in addition a particular triumph: wholeness attained by the transitional woman.
>
> Not only did she learn to stand alone and define herself anew in response to the terrible pressures of a city ghetto; she did so without killing within herself the African woman that she was. Ellen Kuzwayo is not Westernized; she is one of those who has Africanized the Western concept of woman in herself and achieved a synthesis with meaning for all who experience cultural conflict.

Winnie Mandela married Nelson Mandela in June 1958, in the middle of the Treason Trial. During much of the first four years of their marriage, Nelson Mandela was in prison or travelling, and during the last year before being imprisoned for life he was in hiding and underground. While the Mandelas have had little normal married life together, their loyalty to one another has been extraordinary. Over the years Winnie Mandela has emerged as a leader in her own right, inspiring and empowering others by her dauntless courage in disregarding many of the restrictions imposed upon her by the government. She has told her own story in the book *Part of My Soul Went with Him.* The readings that follow are Winnie Mandela's reflections about other women; we will focus more on her and Nelson Mandela in the next session.

Ritual

Ask one member of the group to introduce each of the four women leaders.

Symbolic action: As strong as these four women were, in their writings they show how much strength they drew from solidarity with others. After the readings in this chapter we will use the ancient ritual of anointing with oil to symbolize our own sharing of strength with one another, remembering also the woman who anointed Jesus before his passion (John 12:1-7).

As a small jar of oil is passed around, have people anoint one another on the temple and on the palms of the hands. As practiced in some churches, anointing with oil at baptism and confirmation is accompanied by prayers for strength in continuing our commitment to gospel values. Thus as we anoint one another, let us pray for strength for our minds and strength for the work of our hands. As we put a hand briefly to our own hearts, let us pray for strength in our hearts also.

Scripture:

Luke 1:46-55. The Magnificat
Luke 18:1-8. The Persistent Widow

After reading the Gospel, ask the participants to stand in silence for two minutes with their arms raised and fists closed in the African National Congress salute of strength. As they do this, ask them to reflect on the things that need to be changed before women everywhere live in freedom and dignity.

After the reading of "Twenty thousand strong we marched," ask participants to raise their right arms as they listen to the song, "You have touched the women, you have struck a rock" from the cassette *Rain Upon Dry Land*, by Carolyn McDade. (See Resources.)

To close, create a litany: begin with the names of the four women in this chapter and continue in a litany of thanksgiving for strong women leaders everywhere; encourage participants to name women who have been important in their own lives. Use the response, "O God, we thank you for her strength and courage."

For the next session, ask people to bring a symbol of fidelity—a sign of their own fidelity to another person or group, or of God's faithfulness.

70

Readings

Twenty thousand strong we marched...

I shall never forget what I saw on 9 August 1956—thousands of women standing in silence for thirty minutes, arms raised high in the clenched fist of the Congress salute.

Twenty thousand women of all races from all parts of South Africa were massed together in the huge stone amphitheatre of the Union Buildings in Pretoria, the administrative seat of the government, high on a hill. The brilliant colors of African headscarves, the brightness of Indian saris, and the emerald green of the blouses worn by Congress women merged together in an unstructured design, woven together by the very darkness of those thousands of faces.

Lilian Ngoyi, Rahima Moosa, Sophie Williams and I, Helen Joseph, together with four women from more distant areas, had led the women up to the topmost terrace and into the amphitheatre. I turned my head once as we came marching up. I could see nothing but women following us, thousands of women marching, carrying letters of defiant protest against unjust laws, against the hated pass system, against passes for African women.

We represent and we speak on behalf of thousands of women—women who could not be with us. But all over this country at this moment women are watching and thinking of us. Their hearts are with us.

We are women from every part of South Africa. We are women of every race; we come from the cities and towns, from the reserves and the villages. We come as women united in our purpose to save the African women from the degradation of carrying passes.

Raids, arrests, loss of pay, long hours at the pass office, weeks in the cells awaiting trial, forced farm labor—this is what the pass laws have brought to African men . . . punishment and misery, not for a crime, but for the absence of a pass. We African women know too well the effect of this law on our homes, upon our children. We who are not African women know how our sisters suffer. . . .

We shall not rest until all pass laws and all forms of permits restricting our freedom have been abolished.

We shall not rest until we have won for our children their fundamental rights to freedom, justice and security.

We took those letters of protest into the Union Buildings, to the offices of the prime minister, Johannes Stijdom. He was not there. We flooded his office with them and returned to the thousands of women waiting for us, packed so tightly together, overflowing the amphitheatre. We stood on the little stone rostrum, looking down on the women again, and Lilian called on them to stand in silent protest for thirty minutes. As she raised her right arm in the Congress salute, twenty thousand arms went up and stayed up for those endless minutes.

We knew that all over South Africa in other cities and towns women were gathered in protest. We were not just twenty thousand women; we were many thousands more.

The clock struck three, then a quarter past; it was the only sound. I looked at those many faces until they became only one face, the face of the suffering black people of South Africa. I know that there were tears in my eyes and I think that there were many who wept with me. At the end of that half hour Lilian began to sing, softly at first, "Nkosi Sikilele Afrika" (Lord, give strength to Africa). For blacks it has become the national anthem, and the voices rose, joining Lilian, ever louder and stronger. Then I heard the new song, composed specially for the protest. "You have struck a rock; you have tampered with the women; you shall be destroyed." It was meant for the prime minister, the grim-faced apostle of apartheid and white domination, implacable enemy of the struggle of the black people for freedom and justice.

The protest over the women went away, down the terrace steps, with the same dignity and discipline with which they had come, but now singing. The lovely gardens stood empty again. Yet not really empty, for I think the indomitable spirit remained. Perhaps it is still there, unseen, unheard, unfelt, for the women that day had made the Union Buildings their own.

—Helen Joseph
from *Side by Side*

Nelson's friends

I was influenced by Nelson's friends as I spent more time with these tremendous women, like the late Lilian Ngoyi, whom I greatly admired. She made me, in the sense that I idolized her. There were little ideological differences, but the women who were close to Nelson, whom I was with daily, taught me a great deal. They were just a continuation of Nelson. Albertina Sisulu, Florence Matumela, Ma Frances Baard, Kate Molali and Ruth Mopati, my husband's secretary, who also played a prominent role in my political outlook. These were the people at the top of the ANC hierarchy. I admired them very much and learned from them what the struggle was all about. And of course Helen Joseph, who I have regarded completely as my mother, because of what she has meant to me, not only politically but from a completely human point of view.

—Winnie Mandela
from *Part of My Soul Went with Him*

The tie of friendship

Lilian's earlier bans had expired in 1972 and were not renewed for three years. Friends brought her to see me as soon as she was free and there we were, sitting together on my verandah, as though there had never been ten years silence between us. It had been a bitter time for her but she had survived it. She still seemed ageless; her vitality and her fire were undimmed. She told me of her plans to travel, to go to Durban, to Cape Town, to stay freely in other people's houses again, to catch up on what had been happening during her empty years. We were together again, but we were not going to be able to meet as freely as we should like because she had no transport and as a white I could not go into any African township without a permit. At least we knew that when the opportunities did come, there would be no barriers.

We had worked side by side in the exciting years on the 1950s, had been to jail together, had been on trial for four and a half years for high treason together and had been acquitted together. House arrest and bans had separated us on and off for the past twenty-five years. Only very occasionally had it been possible for us to meet, secretly, but the tie of our friendship has never been broken.

—Helen Joseph
from *Side by Side*

Lilian Ngoyi

Lilian
I hear you are fifty-nine
I've never met you
only seen pictures of you

heard people talk about you
I know you must still be
young and beautiful.

The journalist reports
on the fifteen years
State decree
severing contact
with humanity. . .
You were punished in prison
solitary
alone
when spirit proved rock-like
irrepressed
sentenced to long-term
house arrest. . .

house walls
transformed
into prison walls
house locks
into prison locks—
people forbidden to enter. . .

within the housejail
mind behind
lock and key
fifteen
consecutive
years. . .

within the housejail
dreams permitted
deprived of voice
fifteen
consecutive
years. . .

within the housejail
burned spirit
buried alive
fifteen

consecutive
years. . .

only the police
monitoring
the minutes
of your life
crashing
into your loneliness
at will. . .
seeking
to cut the heart
out of your life-span.

To the journalist
you are a lioness
undaunted
moved to anger
for those
you were unable to help—
this your sole regret. . .

You laugh
weep
shake with rage
your voice dropping
as you explain
"my people are suffering
. . .they suffer."

Listen Lilian
every woman of fifty-nine
should be beautiful
like you.

—A.N.C. Kumalo
from *Poets to the People*

Lilian's death

In 1975 Lilian was banned again, though less severely than before.
She was still forbidden to attend political meetings but she could

communicate with her friends and we met sometimes. The news of her death in 1980 was a great shock to me and I felt a sick rage when I received a telephone call only half an hour after I learned of it. The voice was the usual one, "I hear Lilian Ngoyi has passed away . . . I am so glad." I put the receiver down without speaking.

Her death brought great sorrow to Soweto. "Ma Ngoyi" they called her there. "Ma" is a designation of great respect and love. In her little Orlando home, despite her bans, Lilian had remained a central figure.

I went to Orlando for her funeral, remembering the day we had led twenty thousand women to Pretoria to protest against passes, the day she had called for thirty minutes of motionless silence and then led the women in the singing of "Nkosi Sikelele." At her funeral we sang it again but her voice was silent.

The large church was packed with people and bright with Congress colors. Six women of the Federation and the African National Congress Women's League maintained a guard of honor in their green blouses and black skirts, standing still and silent on each side of the coffin where she lay under the Congress flag.

It was a gathering of the old members of the ANC and the Federation and the Women's League, but they were joined by the young. All differences disappeared and young and old, Black Consciousness and Congress, joined together in tribute. I joined the guard of honor beside the coffin for a little while before the women carried it out of the church, Amina Cachalia's green and yellow sari brilliant among them. A moving announcement had been made. "Lilian Ngoyi lived a life of great simplicity and we shall bury her in simplicity. The coffin will be borne on a cart drawn by two horses."

A thousand people walked behind her, five miles to the cemetary. All the way, the people of Soweto came out of their houses to wave their farewell to her as she passed, giving her the Amandla salute, the clenched fist of strength and struggle.

—Helen Joseph
from *Side by Side*

An unexpected visitor

Ellen Kuzwayo worked with the YWCA for many years and provided a strong presence in many other church groups. Both her sons were actively involved in the black consciousness movement. In October 1977, when the

Christian Institute and all black movements were suddenly banned, Ellen,
at the age of sixty-three, was detained for six months.

I was given a seat across the table facing the man I had presumed
was the leader of the group. The second sat in line with the leader,
but in a corner, with his arms folded across his chest, looking straight
ahead and mute. The third man sat behind me.

Without introducing himself, the "leader" of this trio started telling
me about their mission, namely, that his department was thinking
of releasing me, but before this could happen they had come to
talk to me. I looked up and asked who he was. He replied, "I am
the Minister of Justice." Startled by this disclosure, I responded,
"Are you Mr. Jimmy Kruger?" He nodded, and I continued, "I feel
honored and privileged to speak to you, sir." His reply was that
he too was honored and privileged to speak to a leading member
of the Soweto community. I felt mocked and insulted, and gave
a firm response: "No Minister of Justice would be honored and
privileged to speak to a prisoner." Silence. I continued: "This is
besides the point. What is it you have come to see me about, sir?"

The conversation then became involved. I was told that they
were considering reconstructing the schools program, and so I
should go to Cape Town. My very first reaction to this was that
I was to be banned there, but he reassured me that this was not
the case.

If I was to arrange a holiday at the seaside, my choice would
be to go to Durban to be with my son and his family. I had hardly
completed that statement when the Minister raised both his fisted
hands and banged the table, saying, "That son of yours who gave
the government so much trouble." In a flash I responded, "On the
contrary, the government gave my son unnecessary trouble."

I paused and continued, as I felt it unnecessary to make an issue
out of this matter. "This is besides the point. Can we go on?"

At that point, fear of a longer detention was far from my mind.
Uppermost at that time was the recognition of the fact that I had
been offered the chance of a lifetime, that of a black woman in
South Africa having an interview with the Minister of Justice and
Prisons. It was without precedent, and one which I intended using
to the full. Our interview centered on the need for better
communication between the black people of South Africa and the
Nationalist government, and I let him know of the black
community's long-standing dissatisfaction; that while the state saw
it fitting to plan the future and destiny of our community, the black
people themselves saw this as a futile, sterile exercise; that the
government-chosen leaders could never enter into any meaningful
negotiations with the government on behalf of the blacks because

as state employees they would say only the things the authorities wished to hear. I concluded: "The day the government of this country agrees to sit round the table with the black people's own chosen leaders, then shall we begin to see the dawn of a new day of anticipated peace and calm within our country."

Needless to say, the Minister did not take this at all well and our interview ended. Nevertheless, I felt I had made my mark.

—Ellen Kuzwayo
from *Call Me Woman*

Waiting for friends

8. Keeping Faith: Nelson and Winnie Mandela

Nelson and Winnie Mandela are an extraordinary couple. To the people of South Africa and to many others throughout the world they have become symbols of faithful love: faithful to their people, faithful to the struggle, faithful to each other.

This session celebrates the faithfulness of Nelson and Winnie Mandela at each of these levels. Most of the excerpts that follow are taken from *The Struggle is My Life*, a collection of Nelson Mandela's speeches, and *Part of My Soul Went with Him*. The latter is Winnie Mandela's own story in interviews and letters, edited by Anne Benjamin. Both books include biographical notes and quotations from people who knew the Mandelas before and during Nelson's years in prison.

Ritual

Begin by lighting the candle and observing a few moments of silence. After the readings, say aloud:

> To have and to hold,
> for better, for worse,
> for richer, for poorer,
> in sickness and in health,
> till death do us part.

Reflect on what these marriage vows have meant for Nelson and Winnie Mandela, considering all three levels of their commitment and fidelity.

Reflect on the following questions:

• To whom and to what do we try to be faithful?

- What does faithfulness ask of us?
- What are important signs and symbols of fidelity? (e.g. a ring, a rainbow.) Ask people to place the symbols they have brought around the candle, briefly explaining their significance.
- In what ways have we known the fidelity of God?

Scripture: Isaiah 58:6-12. "Then you shall call, and the Lord will answer."

Close with the singing of the hymn "Be Not Afraid" (This can be found in Vol. I of the *Glory and Praise* hymnal. See page 24).

Readings

The Rivonia Trial, 1962

After the massacre of Sharpeville, the African National Congress turned to armed struggle and formed Umkhonto we Sizwe, "The Spear of the Nation." Their headquarters at Rivonia, outside Johannesburg, were discovered by the police and all the leaders, including Mandela, were brought to trial in 1962. At the trial, Mandela said:

We of the ANC had always stood for non-racial democracy, and we shrank from any action which might drive the races further apart than they already were. But the hard facts were that fifty years of nonviolence had brought the African people nothing but more and more repressive legislation and fewer and fewer rights. It may not be easy for this court to understand, but it is a fact that for a long time the people had been talking of violence—of the day when they would fight the white man and win back the country—and we, the leaders of the ANC, had always prevailed upon them to avoid violence and to pursue peaceful methods.

Mandela's closing words at the Rivonia Trial, just before he received a life sentence:

During my lifetime I have dedicated myself to this struggle of the African people. I have fought against white domination, and I have fought against black domination. I have cherished the ideal of a democratic and free society in which all persons live together in harmony and with equal opportunities. It is an ideal which I hope to live for and to achieve. But if needs be it is an ideal for which I am prepared to die.

from *The Struggle is My Life*

Reprinted by permission of Pathfinder Press. Copyright © 1986 by the International Defence and Aid Fund and Pathfinder Press.

How can I lose hope?

Anne Benjamin writes:

I will never forget my first conversation with Winnie Mandela. A strange intensity made us skip the intermediary phases of getting to know each other, and we touched on some of the vital issues of her life and her experience. Were there not times when she lost all hope and courage? When she felt nothing but resignation and despair?

Her first answer came quickly, with an angry glance: "Of course not. How can I lose hope when I know that in truth this country is ours and that we will get it back—I know that all this is something I must bear in order to reach that goal."

But then she fell silent, and her silence told of the forces against which she must fight continually. And in a husky tone—her voice is usually clear and melodious—she added: "I am too small in this enormous liberation machine. Blacks are dying every day in this cause. Who am I to contribute my little life? The case before us is too great for me to even be thinking of what happens to me personally."

from *Part of My Soul Went with Him*

Wedding

81

A strange married life

From its beginning the Mandelas' married life was strange, bedevilled. Nelson was attending the treason trial day after day, and like me, earning a living by working long hours in addition to the monolithic demands of the trial. He used to join me in my car for the Pretoria run at eight o'clock in the morning. By then he had already put in a couple hours at his law office and by five o'clock in the evening he would be back there again seeing clients, working late into the night before returning home to his bride.

During those first years there can have been little marriage companionship except during trial adjournments, yet that was all that Nelson and Winnie were to have. For the past quarter of a century they have been separated, first by Nelson going underground from the end of the trial and then by his arrest in July of 1962 with the endless years of imprisonment to follow.

Dependent upon snatched meetings, an hour in secret here, a couple of hours there, never daring to meet in their own home, to sit at table with their two little daughters, what sort of life was that on which to build a marriage that must endure through twenty years and more of Robben Island widowhood? For widowhood it is, this pattern of thirty-minute visits at the jail, through a perspex window, speaking through a telephone and always in the presence of a warder.

Winnie has not touched Nelson's hand for the past twenty years. Yet Zindzi, their youngest daughter, declares that they are still so much in love with each other that she feels she ought not intrude on the togetherness that blossoms, even in the jail visiting room.

—Helen Joseph
from *Side by Side*

Winnie's detention

Anne Benjamin writes:

In May 1969 Winnie Mandela and twenty-one men and women were detained in nationwide dawn raids under the Terrorism Act. She was to spend 491 days in detention, most of it in solitary confinement. They were then charged under the Suppression of Communism Act with "furthering the aims of an unlawful organization" [the African National Congress].

She quotes Bishop Manas Buthelezi:

I am happy that Mrs. Mandela was banned too, detained too, and imprisoned too. Her name and stature have forced even some of the most apathetic to realize what is behind the reality of bannings, detentions and political imprisonments. She is a window through which even the most uninitiated eyes are introduced to the obscure, twilight existence of the banned and detained. That is why I say she was a gift of God for us all. She was and is the incarnation of the black people's spirit.

from Part of My Soul Went with Him

Liberated in prison

I got more liberated in prison. The physical identification with your beliefs is far more satisfying than articulating them on a platform. I am not saying it is best to be in prison. But under the circumstances, where it is a question of which prison is better, the prison outside or inside—the whole country is a prison for the black man—and when you are inside, you know why you are there and the people who put you there also know.

from Part of My Soul Went with Him

The horror of detention

The detainees suffered greatly during months of detention, especially during interrogation. Winnie described it years later in a speech during a brief period of freedom.

. . . It means the beginning of that horror told many a time.
. . . It means being held in a single cell with the light bulb burning twenty-four hours so that I lost track of all time and was unable to tell whether it was night or day. . . .The frightful emptiness of those hours of solitude is unbearable. Your company is your solitude, your blanket, your mat, your sanitary bucket, your mug and yourself. . . . All this is in preparation for the inevitable HELL—interrogation. It is meant to crush your individuality entirely, to change you into a docile being from whom no resistance can arise. . . .There have been alleged suicides in detention; you keep asking yourself whether you will leave the cell alive for you do not know what drove those who died to their deaths. . . . Here you have to enter into a debate with yourself. There are only two decisions; you decide whether you will emerge a collaborator with the system or continue your identification with whatever your cause is.

When Winnie and twenty-two others came to trial, the truth of her words was evident. There were some who had been their friends, their colleagues, who went into the witness box to testify against them. Only two had been able to hold out against the horrors of interrogation, had held on to their loyalty.

Acquittal for Winnie and her friends came in 1970. Within minutes, they were re-detained before ever they could leave the court, to spend another six months in solitary confinement. The state eventually brought them ludicrously to trial again on charges so nearly identical with those on which they had been acquitted that the state case was thrown out immediately and they were at last free.

—Helen Joseph
from *Side by Side*

Mandela's confidence

Mac Maharaj, an ANC prisoner who spent twelve years on Robben Island with Nelson Mandela, wrote:

His confidence in the future has been growing. I do not recall a time when he showed any despondence or gave us any clue that he may be thinking in the back of his mind that we would never live through prison. He has always shown this belief in private and in public, and I believe I can say this, knowing him intimately, not even when Winnie was in jail, detained, or when news came out of her torture or whatever demoralizing actions were taken by the enemy, has Nelson flagged. His spirit has been growing, and I think the reasons for this high morale among us are very deeply related to our conditions.

quoted in *The Struggle Is My Life*

Reprinted by permission of Pathfinder Press. Copyright © 1986 by the International Defence and Aid Fund and Pathfinder Press.

The first contact visit

On the weekend of 12 to 13 May 1984, we had our first "contact visit." Can you imagine! We last touched his hand in 1962. When I arrived at Pollsmoor Prison—Zeni and her youngest with me—Sergeant Gregory called me to the office. I got a terrible shock, I thought Nelson was sick, because that's very unusual.

He said: "As from now on you will be able to have different visits. I thought I should bring the news gently to you." We kissed Nelson and held him a long time. It is an experience one just can't put into words. It was fantastic and hurting at the same time.

He clung to the child right through the visit.

Gregory, his warder, was so moved, he looked the other way. That the system could have been so cruel as to deny us that right for the last twenty-two years! Why deny that right to a man who is jailed for life?

from Part of My Soul Went with Him

The birthright of the people

Nelson Mandela's response to the conditional offer of freedom made by P.W. Botha, as introduced and read by his daughter, Zinzi, in Soweto on February 10, 1985:

On Friday my mother and our attorney saw my father at Pollsmoor Prison to obtain his answer to Botha's offer of conditional release. The prison authorities attempted to stop this statement from being made but he would have none of this and made it clear that he would make the statement to you, the people.

My father and his comrades at Pollsmoor Prison send their greetings to you, the freedom-loving people of this our tragic land, in the full confidence that you will carry on the struggle for freedom. He and his comrades at Pollsmoor Prison send their very warmest greetings to Bishop Desmund Tutu. Bishop Tutu has made it clear to the world that the Nobel Peace Prize belongs to you who are the people. We salute him.

My father and his comrades at Pollsmoor Prison are grateful to the United Democratic Front, who without hesitation made this venue available to them so that they could speak to you today. My father says:

"I am a member of the African National Congress. I have always been a member of the African National Congress and I will remain a member of the African National Congress until the day I die. Oliver Tambo is much more than a brother to me. He is my greatest friend and comrade for nearly fifty years. If there is anyone among you who cherishes my freedom, Oliver Tambo cherishes it more, and I know that he would give his life to see me free. There is no difference between his views and mine.

"I am surprised at the conditions that the government wants to impose on me. I am not a violent man. My colleagues and I wrote in 1952 to [Prime Minister] Malan, asking for a round table conference to find a solution to the problems of our country, but that was ignored. When [Prime Minister] Strijdom was in power, we made the same offer. Again it was ignored. When [Prime Minister] Verwoerd was in power we asked for a national convention for all the people of South Africa to decide on their future. This, too, was in vain.

"It was only then, when all other forms of resistance were no longer open to us, that we turned to armed struggle. Let [current Prime Minister] Botha show that he is different to Malan, Strijdom and Verwoerd. Let him renounce violence. Let him say that he will dismantle apartheid. Let him unban the people's organization, the African National Congress. Let him free all who have been imprisoned, banished or exiled for their opposition to apartheid. Let him guarantee free political activity so that people may decide who will govern them.

"I cherish my own freedom dearly, but I care even more for your freedom. Too many have died since I went to prison. Too many have suffered for the love of freedom. I owe it to their widows, to their orphans, to their mothers and to their fathers who have grieved and wept for them. Not only I have suffered during these long, lonely wasted years. I am not less life-loving than you are. But I cannot sell my birthright nor the birthright of the people to be free. I am in prison as the representative of the people and of our organization, the African National Congress, which was banned.

"What freedom am I being offered while the organization of the people remains banned? What freedom am I being offered when I may be arrested on a pass offence? What freedom am I being offered to live my life as a family with my dear wife, who remains in banishment in Brandfort? What freedom am I being offered when I must ask permission to live in an urban area? What freedom am I being offered when I need a stamp in my pass to seek work? What freedom am I being offered when my very South African citizenship is not respected?

"I cannot and will not give any undertaking at a time when I and you, the people, are not free.

"Your freedom and mine cannot be separated. I will return."

And I Watch It in Mandela

It is not to wait until the sky is blue
To turn, look up and see new light.
The sky has turned the colors of violence
For centuries of the agony of the land below it,
And the centuries of truth in the land before it
Bloom only in the flush of new light.

There is fire here;
It is warm;
I am warm,
And I'm comforted.

It has been for this man's life
To paint the new light in the sky.
In all the days when hatred burned
And with its darkness hid the blue,
And in the days to come when black smoke billows still,
This man looks to the deed in the sky.

There is fire here;
It is hot;
I am inflamed.
And I'm heartened.

It is not for the safety of silence
That this man has opened his arms to lead.
The strength of his words hangs in the air
As the strength in his eyes remains on the sky;
And the years of impatient waiting draw on
While this man burns to clear the smoke in the air.

There is fire here,
Which no prison
Can kill in this man;
And I watch it in Mandela.

—John Matshikazi
from *Poets to the People*

9. Prison Experience

Many blacks in South Africa are familiar with the inside of a prison. (The pass laws made it almost impossible to avoid being arrested at some time.) But there is no disgrace attached to going to prison for political reasons; in fact, many political prisoners are seen as heroes. Being arrested in South Africa is not the symbolic gesture it sometimes is in the United States or Canada when people are arrested for civil disobedience. Even after one has survived the terrors of interrogation so vividly described by Winnie Mandela, day-to-day conditions are tough. Yet the New Testament shows us through many disciples' lives that Christians could expect prison if they were really true to their faith.

Ritual

Begin by lighting the candle and turning out the lights for a few moments of darkness. Then read the following lines from a poem by Dennis Brutus, written from the prison on Robben Island:

> ... in the grey of the empty afternoons
> it is not uncommon
> to find oneself talking to God

After the readings, sing "Kumbayah" as the response to the following litany.

A Litany on Human Suffering

All: Someone's crying, Lord, Kumba yah... (sung)

Reader: Someone's crying, Lord, somewhere
Some is millions, somewhere is many places
There are tears of suffering

There are tears of weakness and disappointment
There are the tears of the rich, and the tears of the poor.
Someone's crying, Lord, redeem the times.

All: Someone's dying, Lord, Kumba yah . . . (sung)

Reader: Some are dying of hunger and thirst
Someone is dying because somebody else is enjoying
Too many unnecessary and superfluous things
Someone is dying because people go on exploiting one
another.
Some are dying because there are structures and
systems
Which crush the poor and alienate the rich
Someone is dying, Lord
Because we are still not prepared to take sides
To make a choice, to be a witness
Someone's dying, Lord, redeem the times.

All: Someone's shouting, Lord, Kumba yah . . . (sung)

Reader: Someone's shouting loudly and clearly
Someone has made a choice
Someone is ready to stand up against the times
Someone is shouting out
Offering his or her very existence in love and anger
To fight death surrounding us
To wrestle with the evils with which we crucify each
other.
Someone is shouting, Lord, redeem the times.

All: Someone's praying, Lord, Kumba yah . . . (sung)

Reader: Someone's praying, Lord
We are praying in tears and anger
In frustation and weakness
In strength and endurance
We are shouting and wrestling
As Jacob wrestled with the angel
And was touched
And was marked
And became a blessing
We are praying, Lord
Spur our imagination
Sharpen our political will
Through Jesus Christ you have let us know where you
want us to be.

89

From Let's Worship *(World Council of Churches: 1975).*
Used at a memorial service for June 16, 1986 by the Alliance
of Black Reformed Christians of South Africa

Scripture: Matthew 10:11-20, 24-31, 41-42. "You will be dragged
before governors and kings. . . ."

After a pause, invite anyone who wishes to read again any phrase
from this Scripture that would have special relevance for Christians
in the struggle in South Africa.

> Jesus let all the powers that diminish and bind, that exploit
> and enforce, that deceive and lie, have him. He let them do
> what they could. He let himself be arrested, spit at, detained,
> tortured, ridiculed, and killed. But after that death, he opened
> his eyes, not blind anymore; he opened his hands, not bound
> anymore; he stretched his body, not kept anymore; he opened
> his mouth, not gagged anymore; and he said: "I have passed
> through it all. Evil, where is your power? Satan, where is your
> might? Death, where is your sting?"

> *—Joseph Donders*
> *(former professor of religion and philosophy at the*
> *University of Nairobi)*

The central message of the gospel is that new life can come through
death, and that suffering endured for the sake of love can be a
source of grace. As Jesus said, "Greater love has no one than this,
that one lay down one's life for a friend." (John 15:13)

Symbolic action: Arrange in advance to have several members of
the group act as "police." The rest are asked to do what they are
told to do quietly. The "police" go to several people, make them
close their eyes, tie their wrists together with a short length of
rope, and take them out to the next room, where they are left sitting
on chairs with their eyes closed. When two or three people have
been taken, someone starts to sing, "Were you there when they
crucified my Lord?" This experience can give people new insight
into what it means to live in fear of arrest. However it is important
to know the group well before including this action. Do not let
it go on too long, and be sure to provide an opportunity for people
to discuss afterwards how it felt to be taken, to see others taken
and do nothing about it, or to be the "police." This action is not
advisable for people who have experienced life in a country where
arrests and torture are a daily reality.

Practical action: Contact Amnesty International for names and addresses of prisoners of conscience in South Africa, and correspond with them.

Prayer: Let us ask God for the blessings we hope will come to South Africa and to the whole world as a result of the great love with which so many people in so many lands have risked freedom and life for the sake of their friends. Invite spontaneous prayers in which people may share those signs and symbols that most help them to believe that life does come through death.

Readings

Robben Island

Robben Island—notorious political prison, one-time leper colony, World War II naval fortress—a tiny outcrop of limestone, bleak, windswept and caught in the wash of the icy Benguella current from the Antarctic. It is an island crisscrossed with subterranean tunnels which were constructed as part of its fortifications and it has camouflaged heavy artillery facing outward towards the Atlantic Ocean. It is an island whose history counts the years of bondage of the black man in South Africa and it has been the home of Nelson Mandela for more than a decade and a half. In the early 1960s, when Verwoerd served as the white Premier and Vorster was his Minister of Justice, the island was once more re-established as a political prison. By incarcerating Nelson Mandela and other freedom fighters there they hoped to wipe their names from the lips of the people of South Africa, to bury them living into oblivion.

But the name of Nelson Mandela lives on in the hearts and minds of his people and of all democrats throughout the world. . . .

Within his lifetime Nelson has become a living legend and the people, through their actions, give the lie to the designs of the race-mad ruler of South Africa.

Since early 1976 South Africa has once more been in the throes of a rising tide of revolt. In the wave of uprisings that swept across the country thousands of militants, especially young militants, have been gunned down by the police and the army, whisked away by the Security Police into detention without trial to be tortured, interrogated and in many cases murdered, while others have been brought before the racist courts charged for daring to rise in revolt.

> —Mac Maharaj
> quoted in *The Struggle Is My Life*

Reprinted by permission of Pathfinder Press. Copyright © 1986 by the International Defence and Aid Fund and Pathfinder Press.

Women prisoners in the Johannesburg "Fort"

We had sixteen days in the Fort before we were brought back to court, by now 156 alleged traitors in all. In the women's jail we settled down fairly comfortably in a large cell. We became six when Ruth First joined us some days later. On one of the days we prowled around outside the cell, for once not under the eye of a wardress, and we came upon our black sisters. They were sitting on the stone floor in dark iron sheds. The doors were open and we saw that they had only mats to sleep on and no other furniture. We had time only to exchange loving greetings before we scurried back to our quarters, but we had seen enough to realize with shame how much better off we were in our large light cell with beds and a couple of chairs, even a cupboard. It was a bitter memory, despite the joy of actually seeing them.

—Helen Joseph
from *Side by Side*

Bringing up kids in a prison cell

This was part of a report published in December 1984 by the Institute of Criminology at the University of Cape Town.

I am twenty-eight years old and was arrested in 1981 and 1982 because I do not have a pass to live in Cape Town. I was convicted in the commissioner's court.

The last time I went to prison my children were about four years old and two years old. Both times I was arrested my children accompanied me to jail. Both children were ill with vomiting and diarrhea. I was allowed to take them to the prison hospital but the nurse did not give them the right medicine.

There were many of us in the cell. . . about thirty or forty.

There were no benches and we were each given a mat and two blankets for sleeping. We slept on the cold cement floor as there were no beds.

During the day we cleaned our cell and the rest of the prison. The children stayed with us all the time. I would tie the baby on my back and the older one would just stand next to me.

We never went outside for the whole of five weeks.

The warders confiscated the food I took with me to prison. I do not think friends were allowed to bring food or clothing. So we had no change of clothing, apart from one napkin for the baby which I had to give back when I left.

We were woken at 5 a.m. and had a short time to wash ourselves and the babies. There was no hot water. We fastened blankets with safety pins around us while we washed our clothes and waited for them to dry. We had to hang them on the windows of our cells or spread them over the mats on the floor to dry.

In the morning we had mealie meal, skim milk, a little bread and black coffee with no sugar.

At lunchtime, we ate mealie rice, usually with a little meat. We had vegetables once a week and no fruit at all.

In the evenings, we had porridge, mealie meal, coffee and a slice of dry bread, although sometimes it was spread with fat.

I think the time in prison was hard on the children. The baby had bronchitis by the time I was released. We received far too little food and if we asked for more food it was refused. We also needed more blankets.

—from *Vukani Makhosikhazi*

A Poem Written from Prison on Robben Island

Particularly in a single cell,
but even in the sections
the religious sense assets itself;

perhaps a childhood habit of nightly prayers
the accessibility of Bibles,
or awareness of the proximity of death:

and, of course, it is a currency—
pietistic expressions can purchase favors
and it is a way of suggesting reformation
(which can produce promotion);

and the resort of the weak
is to invoke divine revenge
against a rampaging injustice;

but in the grey of the empty afternoons
it is not uncommon
to find oneself talking to God.

—Dennis Brutus
from *Letters to Martha and Other Poems*

Ten thousand children detained in 1986 "emergency"

Since a new state of emergency was declared on June 12, 1986, it is reckoned by the Detainee's Parents Support Committee, considered the most reliable source of information, that thirty thousand people have been detained, and that forty percent of these have been children under eighteen . . . .

On June 11, the day before the new state of emergency was declared—Patrick Makhoba says he was with six friends on the grounds of his high school in Soweto when the police appeared. "We had no way of running," he remembers, "they were everywhere. The school was surrounded. I couldn't believe so many people would come for seven little boys. I was sixteen." He is small with a sprinkling of freckles over his nose. But he was hardly an innocent in the ways of life in South African townships. When the police swooped down on his school he was already carrying his toothbrush. He no longer slept at home every night, preferring to evade security forces by sleeping in different houses on different nights.

He says he was beaten at the schoolyard and later, at the police station in Soweto, was interrogated and beaten again. "We were told not to lean against anything and we were so tired. We were lined up and they would come in and look at us and then just kick one of us."

He was kept in solitary confinement for thirty-nine days. "I couldn't even see the sun," says Makhoba. But there was a window so he could tell the passing of the days. There were interrogations as well as questions about student organizations, about who was responsible for student demonstrations. Sometimes in the interrogation room, "They would handcuff me and push me against a wall and push a table against me so I couldn't move, then someone would jump on the table and help himself to me—just beat me, beat me in the face."

After forty-two days in jail, "They just came in and said, 'Pack your bags and go.' I did it, but I didn't show any happiness. I thought, 'I am not going to believe it.' And I didn't believe it until I got to my mother's house."

—adapted from an article by Carla Hall in the
International Herald Tribune, June 30, 1987

10. The Struggle Towards Unity

Power and privilege have created a deep chasm between whites and blacks in South Africa. In order to maintain its power, the white minority has done everything possible to divide blacks among themselves, Indians from so-called "Coloureds," "Coloureds" from Africans, Zulus from Swazis, Basotho from Xhosas, etc. Worst of all has been the division created by blacks who have been co-opted to work within the system through homelands governments and community councils, in the police force and through the extensive network of government informers. These people have become the enemies of those committed to the total dismantling of apartheid in a new non-racial society.

Blacks know that in order to defeat apartheid they must be united. They have struggled long and hard to achieve the unity that exists in spite of government machinations to divide them. The signing of the Freedom Charter; the 1983 establishment of the United Democratic Front (UDF), a coalition of anti-apartheid groups; and the organization of the Congress of South African Trade Unions (COSATU) have all been major triumphs.

Ritual

Scripture: Ephesians 2:12-16. Jesus has broken down the dividing wall of hostility.

The Christian church has often seen its position as that of reconciler between people in disagreement. This view is challenged, however, in the 1986 Kairos Document, signed by many prominent South African church leaders. They maintain that the role of reconciler is inadequate in a situation of tyranny such as that in South Africa. (The historical importance of the Kairos Document is explained in the following chapter. An analysis is found in *South Africa's Moment of Truth,* Chapter Eight.)

Symbolic Action: Lead the group through a guided action-meditation. Ask everyone to stand, close their eyes and clasp their hands behind their backs. They are to reflect for a moment on themselves as unique individuals, giving thanks for the ways they enjoy total autonomy and recognizing at the same time the ways they feel isolated. Then ask them to open their eyes and to form a small group with those with whom they have such natural bonds as age, sex, race, culture, family, etc. (Some may have to make a choice between several different bonds.) It does not matter if the groups are of different sizes, but if there are more than five people in a group it should break into groups of three.

Ask the members of each of the groups to discuss the following: What do they enjoy in one another's company? What do they have to bring to the larger community? How might they be hindering unity in the larger community? Then split up the groups and ask people to form new groups of three, each person coming from a different group. Have them share the points that were made in their previous group's discussion.

Finally, ask them to discuss which groups are not present at all in this gathering, and why? What could be done to develop deeper understanding and closer bonds with other groups in the community? Ask the whole group to form a circle by holding hands and to name the groups that are not present, suggesting ways to establish contact with them, e.g. by inviting them to the final gathering in the series.

Close with the hymn, "Bind us together, God, bind us together with cords that cannot be broken," or another appropriate hymn.

Readings

... as a human being

In much of South Africa, with anybody who is white, we maintain that master-servant relationship. So when you meet someone as a human being, it's such a jubilation.

—from the introduction to *South Africa: Time Is Running Out*

How shall we fashion a land of peace?

Yes, there are a hundred, and a thousand voices crying. But what does one do, when one cries this thing, and one cries another? Who knows how we shall fashion a land of peace where black outnumber white so greatly? Some say that the earth has bounty enough for all, and that more for one does not mean less for another. They say that poor-paid labor means a poor nation, and that better-paid labor means greater markets and greater scope for industry and manufacture. And others say that this is a danger. For better-paid labor will not only buy more but will read more, think more, ask more, and will not be content to be forever voiceless and inferior.

Who knows how we shall fashion such a land? For we fear not only loss of our possessions, but the loss of our superiority and the loss of our whiteness. Some say it is true that crime is bad, but would this not be worse? Is it not better to hold what we have, and to pay the price of it with fear? And others say, can such fear be endured? For is it this fear that drives men to ponder these things at all?

—Alan Paton
from *Cry, the Beloved Country*

The Whiteman Blues

Two cars, three loos, a swimming pool,
Investment painting, kids at a private school . . .
we entertain with shows or gourmet food—
and yet we don't feel right, we don't feel good.

Why doesn't the having help?
Why doesn't the spending save?
Why doesn't the fun—
Why doesn't the culture—
Why don't the ads add up to something?

We can afford to say we know
the blacks are really given hell,
Big Boss is harsh and stupid and must go:
we say it—and it helps like one Aspro.
We still feel jumpy, mixed up, not quite well.

Which specialist can cure the thing we've got—
the got-ta, gotta-get-it blues,
the deep-freeze, cheaper wholesale, world excursion blues?
We're high on the know-all-about-it booze.

We're bursting with kwashiorkor* of the bank.
We're depressed by the whiteman blues.

In the backyards they pray for us.
In Soweto they see our plight.
In the border areas they understand.
In the Bantustans they wait
to pat our shoulders, hold our hand.
They know, they know,
to them it isn't news:
we've got those lost-man, late-man,
money-man, superman,
whiteman blues.

> —Lionel Abrahams
> from *Modern South African Poetry*

The privilege and pain of being white

I drove back alone to Johannesburg, to my comfortable home in a white suburb, to my comfortable white life, my well-paid white job and it all seemed unreal. Lilian's bitter cry, "You are better off with your skin" was haunting me again. I had accepted my whiteness for so many years, ever since I came to South Africa. I had accepted that whites, simply because of the color of their skins, lived on a higher socio-economic scale. It was for the eradication of this utterly invalid privilege that I was now fighting. The experience of the last few years, particularly the treason trial and the search for the banished, had begun to make me ashamed of being what I was and it made no difference that I did not choose to be white. I am white and I live a more comfortable life because I do not or cannot break out of my whiteness.

> —Helen Joseph
> from *Side by Side*

Sowing seeds of mistrust

It would have made a great deal of difference if we had been released at the same time. I often wonder whether these are calculated moves

---

* Severe protein-calorie malnutrition in children, one of the signs of which is a swollen belly.

by those in authority to sow the seeds of mistrust among the detainees. The obvious outcome for those left behind is to start asking questions within and among themselves: Why has so and so been released? Why not me? Why not us? All the same, I have reason to believe that there is great awareness within the ranks of those black people of the kind of psychological tactics used by the police.

Other moves which can create suspicion within the black "leadership" (I use this word with reservation to mean those people the masses often look up to, even if they are not vocal or in the forefront of community events) include suddenly granting a passport to someone who has been branded a troublemaker, while those who were similarly branded are denied a passport. The community raises their eyebrows and asks, "Why him? Why not us?" Certain circles in the black community are well aware of this attempt to divide us. Let us all be warned.

—Ellen Kuzwayo
from *Call Me Woman*

Those at the top—those below

Nozizwe*

You were to be the center of our dream
To give life to all that is abandoned.
You were to heal the wound
To restore the bones that were broken.
But you betrayed us!
You chose a lover from the enemy
You paraded him before us like a sin.
You dared embrace the killer of your father
You led your clans to the gallows.
You mocked the gods of our Forefathers.
You shouted our secrets before the little strangers
You mocked the sacred heads of our elders
You cast down their grey hair before the children
Their lips that hold the ancient truths were sealed.
By their sunken eyes your body was cursed
The moving river shall swallow it!

> —Mazisi Kunene
> from *The Ancestors and the Sacred Mountain*

An Agony

My head is heavy, my shoulders shrug,
because despite
all my eyes have seen
my head has said
my heart has felt,
I do not believe
that White, Black and Yellow
cannot, walk, talk, eat, kiss and share.
It worries me to think
that only people of my color
will liberate me.

You mustn't trust a white man
my grandfather used to tell me
when I was a child.

* A traitor who served the South African police

You mustn't think that a white man cares for you
my people cautioned me.
You know when a white man wants to know you?
When you bring him money.

The Indian? He's black as you.
But, not as poor as you.
He knows his trade—cheating you.
He's happy to lend you money
just forgets to mention
the twenty percent interest!
Until you have to pay it.

And Coloured? I ask
Ag! him, they say.
He doesn't know where he stands,
but, he prefers his skin whitest
and his hair straightest.
And somehow forgets the second names
of his black and kinky cousins!

I know of whites, Coloureds and Indians
who are like that, I say.
But, I'm told they are only a few.

Now, what about you my fellow African?
We are intimidated, they say,
Modimo, we're very very busy, they say,

not losing
our passes,
our birth certificates,
our train tickets,
our rent receipts,
our urban residential permits,
(not to mention our money, our husbands and
our lives).

My head is heavy, my shoulders shrug,
because despite
all my eyes have seen
my head has said
my heart has felt,

I do not believe
that White, Black and Yellow
cannot walk, talk, eat, kiss, and share.

> —Joyce Sikakane
> from *The Return of the Aamasi Bird*

The ANC is committed to non-racialism

The ANC is committed to non-racialism. The ANC cannot imagine a situation in which the white man does not exist. We never look at people as black or white; it is the enemy who compels us to use those terms. The umbrella organization of the ANC embodies everyone who is fighting side by side with us against oppression. The white student at Wits* or Cape Town University who is beaten up by the same system that is beating up my people here in the Free State—must I ignore him? He is fighting the same cause as me. That is a fellow comrade. And you can't ignore those students who today are so brave as to hold anti-Republic demonstrations with a vacant chair labelled "Nelson Mandela." They are fellow human beings who are fighting side by side in our struggle. The South Africa of tomorrow that I'm fighting for will include the white child who has been so brave defying his Broederbond parents and shouting slogans of my movement on the campus. I can't ignore him. He is part of us.

There are certain whites—Bram Fischer, Helen Joseph, Goldberg, Beyers Naude—you would never dream of thinking of them in terms of color. Those whites, who are white in the law, are to us comrades and fellow freedom-fighters. I have as much respect for Helen Joseph as for my mother Lilian Ngoyi. I get a shock when I am reminded that they are white. They are part of us, of the cause, of our suffering. We are determined to create a harmonious racial situation in this country, including the white South African, the white student.

> —Winnie Mandela
> from *Part of My Soul Went with Him*

---

* The University of Witwatersrand

11. The Witness of Christian Leaders

For many years, mainline South African churches were dominated by whites and remained out of touch with the lives of black people. By the 1950s and 60s, many bright young Africans felt that the church was totally irrelevant to their lives. Recently, however, there has been a succession of Christian leaders, both black and white, whose faith and loving commitment to people literally shines like a "torch in the night." The risks they have taken and the sacrifices they have made have given credibility to the church's claim that Christ really did bring good news to the poor.

Ritual

If the weather and the situation make it feasible, have the group go outside into the night after reading the paraphrase of Psalm 126 by the Rev. Zephania Kameeta (see Dedication). Once outside, reread selections from *The Night Keeps Winking* (found in various chapters), reflecting on South Africa's hideous night, but recalling the constant whistling, whispering and winking of the stars.

> The bright eye of the night keeps whispering
>   when it paves and pages the clouds
> it is knowledgeable about hideous nights
>   when it winks and keeps winking
> I feel looked at
>   walking in this night
> in this strange land which mutes screams
> The night
>   with its bright eye-ball
> which bears boot prints and flags
>   tells about days which came and went
>   this I know

and the night knows it too
so

the bright eye of the night keeps whispering and whispering
and the stars
with their distance
keep whistling and whistling

—Mongane Serote
from *The Night Keeps Winking*

Light a large candle. Explain to people that most of the poems and stories in this book are about the struggle of blacks in South Africa. Many have been moved to action and strengthened within it by their Christian faith. We want to name some of these men and women. Along with them, we would also like to name a few of the hundreds of white Christians in South Africa who have committed themselves totally to the struggle for a just society and who have built important bridges across the chasms of mistrust.

In the light of the candle, using different readers, begin the following litany (if possible, give each person a copy):

Litany of Thanksgiving for a Long List of Brave Christians

O God, we thank you for the thousands of blacks who have been willing to risk prison, interrogation and death to free your people. We thank you also for their long willingness to forgive those who have wronged them.

Response: O God, we see in them your glory. *(Repeat this after each prayer)*

We thank you for the leadership of Nelson Mandela, Walter Sisulu, Govan Mbeki and all those who have spent years on Robben Island and in other prisons as a result of their commitment to set their people free.

We give you thanks for the life of Alan Paton, who showed his love for black South Africans in his book *Cry, the Beloved Country*, and started to open the hearts and minds of many to the suffering blacks still endure.

We thank you for Chief Albert Luthuli, who won the Nobel Prize for his courageous commitment to peace, but spent the last years of his life in lonely banishment.

We give you thanks for Michael Scott, the priest who first took the plight of the Herero people of Namibia to the United Nations.

We give thanks for Bishop Trevor Huddleston, the author of *Naught for Your Comfort*, who symbolized for the people of Sophiatown your loving commitment as they were forced to give up their homes.

We give thanks for the leadership of Archbishop Hurley, who has built up the commitment of the Catholic Church in South Africa to the struggle for justice.

We give you thanks for the life of Bishop Mandlenkhosi Zwane of Swaziland, who educated the Catholic bishops through a three-day teach-in with alienated young black radicals.

We give you thanks for Cosmas Desmond, who went to Limehill to help the people put up their tents when they were forced to move from their homes in the dead of winter, and who gave this international publicity in his book, *The Discarded People*.

We give you thanks for two Anglican bishops, Geoffrey Clayton and Ambrose Reeves, who were deported because they dared to criticize the government.

We thank you for Bishop David Russell, who as a young priest was banned and imprisoned for his commitment to the poor, living himself on the inadequate food which could be bought with an old-age pension for blacks.

We thank you for Beyers and Ilse Naudé, Afrikaners who have been on a very long spiritual journey as they listened in faith to what God was saying to the churches through hurt and angry people. Their faith and courage have won them the trust of people of all races.

We thank you for the Rev. Allan Boesak—brave community leader, co-founder of the UDF, theologian, president of the World Alliance of Reformed Churches; he challanged those churches to declare apartheid a heresy.

We thank you for Bishop Manas Buthelezi, the Lutheran who first challenged black Christians to a mission to save the souls of white Christians.

We thank you for Barbara Hogan, whose Christian commitment to justice led her to support the ANC. Though she was only involved in peaceful activities she is now serving a ten-year prison sentence.

We give you thanks for Lilian Ngoyi and Ellen Kuzwayo for their commitment to you and to the cause of African women.

We thank you for Sheena Duncan and her mother, Jean Sinclair, both of whom have given outstanding leadership to the Black Sash in its protest against unjust laws and in its legal advice centers for Africans.

We thank you for Steve Biko and all those who restored our appreciation of the beauty of all the different races you have created.

We thank you for Dr. Mamphela Ramphele, who used the lonely years of her banning in Tzaneen (a small town in the eastern Transvaal) to set up a remarkable community health program for the local people.

We thank you for Neil Aggett, a young white doctor who left his profession in order to serve the emergent trade unions and died after torture in detention. Twenty thousand people, mostly black, attended his funeral.

We thank you for Joan and Jimmy Stewart, who started Transformation Center in Lesotho, a place of warmth and friendship for exiles and refugees.

We thank you for Sister Bernard Ncube, who said at a meeting at the Johannesburg Cathedral in May, 1986, "No one should criticize these young comrades. They show more courage and love for one another than any of us have ever done. I spend all my time taking them to hospital and prison." Within a month she was arrested and is still in prison [November 1987].

We thank you for the Hunter family, especially for Roland, who risked passing information about South African support for the rebel MNR forces to the government of Mozambique, and is now serving a five-year jail sentence, and for Catherine, whose leadership in the Young Christian Students movement led to four months in solitary confinement.

We thank you for all those actively committed to nonviolent resistance, and for all the conscientious objectors who risk six years imprisonment if they refuse compulsory service in the South African Defense Force.

We thank you for Albert Nolan, the Dominican theologian whose involvement with Young Christian Students has enabled thousands to see the relevance of Jesus to the situation in South Africa.

We thank you for Father Smangaliso Mkatschwa, the general secretary of the South African Catholic Bishops Conference, who was tortured in 1986 while he was in detention, but maintains his infectious warmth and joy in life.

We thank you for the Rev. Frank Chikane, the new general secretary of the South African Council of Churches, who has frequently been detained and interrogated for his work in drawing together the Kairos Document.

We thank you for Bishop Desmond Tutu, who has used the publicity of the Nobel Peace Prize to focus the attention of the world on the suffering of South Africa, and who has risked his own life trying to prevent violence.

Close the litany with spontaneous prayers for the Christian community in South Africa and for the coming of God's Kingdom. Continue, indoors if necessary, with the readings.

Closing Prayer: All light small candles from the large candle. In silence let us become conscious of the hope that is in the people of South Africa, and share with them our hope:

Brave people of South Africa,
we pray that you keep up your hope
and that you may know that God is with you in the struggle
for a new world of justice and peace.

Readings

Steve Biko challenges church priorities

The church and its operation in modern-day South Africa has to be looked at in terms of the way it was introduced in this country. Even at this late stage, one notes the appalling irrelevance of the interpretation given to the Scriptures. In a country teeming with injustice and fanatically committed to the practice of oppression, intolerance and blatant cruelty because of racial bigotry; in a country where all black people are made to feel the unwanted stepchildren of a God whose presence they cannot feel; in a country where father and son, mother and daughter alike develop daily into neurotics through sheer inability to relate the present to the future because of a completely engulfing sense of destitution, the church further adds to their insecurity by its inward-directed definition of the concept of sin and its encouragement of the *mea culpa* attitude.

Stern-faced ministers stand on pulpits every Sunday to heap loads of blame on black people in townships for their thieving, house-breaking, stabbing, murdering, adultery, etc. No one ever attempts to relate all these vices to poverty, unemployment, overcrowding, lack of schooling and migratory labor. No one wants to completely condone abhorrent behavior, but it frequently is necessary for us to analyze situations a little bit deeper than the surface suggests.

Because the white missionary described black people as thieves, lazy, sex-hungry, etc., the churches, through our ministers, see all these vices mentioned above not as manifestations of the cruelty and injustice which we were subjected to by the white man, but as inevitable proof that, after all, the white man was right when he described us as savages. Thus if Christianity in its introduction was corrupted by the inclusion of aspects which made it the ideal religion for the colonialization of people, nowadays, in its interpretation, it is the ideal religion for the maintenance of the subjugation of the same people.

—Steve Biko
from *I Write What I Like*

Dialogue

Archbishop Hurley speaks of his involvement in protest

. . . the Sharpeville massacre in 1960 stimulated me to do more with the Durban branch of Race Relations. But I was still mostly making speeches. It was through women—members of the Black Sash—that I learned about demonstrating. When an Indian was detained in Durban and committed "suicide" from a prison window, we had a big demonstration here. I felt nervous the first day. Later, I became intrigued by demonstrating—by the way people stared at me, taking a sneaky look, then ducking away.

In the late 1960s Hurley was invited by Cosmas Desmond, a young Catholic priest, to Limehill, a resettlement village of "discarded people." Black families had simply been dumped in the bare veld where there was nothing but a pile of folded tents and a water tank some distance away. He described his visit:

They even took a picture of me driving in a tent peg. More important, I was getting to know people. They were dying, like flies, of an epidemic—especially the children. One afternoon, we counted ninety little graves. We sent their names to the Bantu[*] Administration—which never answered the letter. I was recognizing these people as beings who were suffering enormously. Also, there was a certain excitement in taking action.

One night in Milan, going over a speech I was to give in Germany, I suddenly realized that I myself was part of an oppressive people. They were oppressors, and I was one of them. It was a terrible feeling. It may seem strange that it took so long to realize, to feel this. But that is South Africa. . . .But Christians must never yield to pessimism, no matter how "correctly" the judgement is calculated. And the essential task of the church remains that of giving practical expression to Christian faith. The real test of hope is when the situation is hopeless.

> —Archbishop Denis Hurley
> from *The South African Churches in a Revolutionary Situation*

Manas Buthelezi reverses mission

In 1973 Dr. Manas Buthelezi created a stir when he proposed six provocative theses to the South African Congress on Mission and Evangelism. A central theme was that the future of the Christian faith in South Africa depended largely on how the gospel proved itself relevant to the existential problems of blacks, inasmuch as South African Christendom was predominantly black. Whites had eroded the power of Christian love. Hence for the sake of the survival of the Christian faith it was urgently necessary that blacks step in to save the situation. Indeed, it was time for blacks to evangelize and humanize whites. . . .

Buthelezi's views began to turn the world of the churches upside down. He demanded a new maturity of black Christians—that they not only live out their faith in ways which liberated them psychologically, spiritually and politically from oppression, but that they work simultaneously for the conversion and liberation of whites. For Buthelezi it was partly a matter of agreeing with his colleagues in the Christian Institute that whites had betrayed their

---

[*] Literally, "people" (pl.) in many African languages. Because the term has been used by the South African government to mean "African" it is resented and ridiculed by blacks.

Christian mission, failed to offer Christian fellowship, grabbed the country's wealth and were now threatened by the coming wrath of God. Certainly the church in South Africa had witnessed "the systematic apostasy of the white man." This lack of stewardship (and Buthelezi suggested that selfless Christian stewardship might have given white presence some legitimacy) had "violated the integrity of God's love and justice." Whites had ignored the call to an equitable distribution of resources which was inherent in the Covenant, and likewise ignored the "communal life of sharing . . . [the] communism of the New Testament Church." Like his colleagues in the Christian Institute, Buthelezi argued that in the face of "this spiritual vandalism" the church had to promote its constituency and "cease to be a satellite of white power politics in order to become a forum of communion for the whole people of God." But it was at this point in his analysis that Buthelezi went on to break new ground in demanding of black Christians that they bear the full responsibility of their faith. Black people had not preached the Gospel to all nations—not yet. Rather they seemed to "have been conditioned into thinking of themselves as third-grade kaffir ambassadors of Christ." Had it ever occurred to the black man that if white people are lost . . . he may be held responsible? . . . God will ask: "Black man, where were you when the white man abandoned my Gospel and went to destruction?" When the black man answers, "I was only a kaffir, how could I dare to preach to my master?" God will say: "Was Christ's resurrection not sufficient to liberate you, black man, from that kind of spiritual and psychological death? Go to eternal damnation, black man, for you did not muster courage to save your white brother."

—Peter Walshe
from *Church versus State in South Africa*

Allan Boesak on choosing to be black

Allan Boesak seemed to welcome the chance to talk of his farewell to his early "innocence"—that is, his ignorance of how the bondage of racism determined his daily existence.

Coloured people don't feel completely European or completely African. In my childhood and early youth, I felt I ought to belong to the white Afrikaner community, but felt rejected. I had a longing to be white.

There was also inverted racism in our own community—the lighter ones thought of themselves as better. My own mother looks

110

white, and my father was as dark as any African. Most Coloureds would have tried to neutralize that part—you can imagine the inner conflicts. Fortunately, this kind of tension did not exist in our family. My mother never discriminated among her eight children on account of color. But outsiders, we found, favored the lighter ones in the family.

My father died when I was six, and my mother had to struggle hard as a seamstress to keep the family together. She taught us what it is to care for each other. There's no jealousy between us— the joy of one has always been the joy of the other.

As I grew older, I appreciated her more and also realized that though my black father was only a primary school teacher, he had a great love and understanding of music, art, and poetry. I looked into my family history and learned that the first Boesak—a brown-skinned Khoikhoi—shared with an African the leadership of a slave rebellion. I began to take pride in this, to see myself as the son of the soil. When all things came together, I lost my inferiority feelings. I looked at myself differently. I realized that if I could stop trying to please whites, I could recreate history, so to speak.

In 1973, I spent six months at Union Theological Seminary in the USA. I did research on the ethics of Martin Luther King. And I saw that blacks there could be confident, and have a spontaneous attitude towards whites. Because they accepted their blackness.

All this time black consciousness was growing. Many Coloureds began to realize we're part of a common oppressed community. The whole question of being a Coloured, Indian, or African was not just an ethnic, but a political question. We needed unity in the struggle. We had to make choices.

—Allan Boesak
from *The South African Churches in a Revolutionary Situation*

Kairos—The Moment of Truth

In September 1985, 152 Christians in South Africa, many of them priests and ministers, published the Kairos Document. It was recognized around the world as identifying a new and controversial step in the churches' efforts to identify with the struggle of the poor.

The Kairos Document comes straight out of the flames of South African townships. Those who have no experience of the oppression, the repression, the sufferings and the struggles of the people in the townships will not be able to understand the faith questions that are being put here, let alone the answers. . . .

The Kairos Document was not planned; it just happened. It has mushroomed into something far greater than anyone had anticipated. It continues to be printed, re-printed, translated, distributed, discussed and debated all over the world. There is now a second revised edition. No book or document this century has had such an impact upon Christians. The Kairos Document is not only a milestone in the history of theology in South Africa, it is also a milestone in the whole history of Christian theology. That may appear to be an exaggerated claim but it is what many theologians throughout the world are saying about this remarkable document.

Praise for all of this is not due to the Kairos theologians. Perhaps some praise is due to the oppressed Christians of South Africa and their unshakeable faith. But in the final analysis, praise is due God alone, and to the movement of his spirit that put this challenge, this theological catalyst (with all its possible human errors) into our history at this stage. We can thank God for it because, like all genius theological efforts, it is certainly challenging and nourishing the faith of very many Christians today.

—Albert Nolan, O.P.
from *To Nourish Our Faith*

Reflections on the *kairos* moment

There comes a time in the life of every individual, of every institution, of every community, of every country, when a decision has to be taken in the sphere of what is just or unjust, what is good or what is evil, what leads to life or inevitably brings death. On the outcome of that decision depends the future destiny of the individual or the group which has to make that decision. In biblical times, the term used was *kairos*, the moment of truth. And usually, such a moment is brought about either by a single crisis in the life of such an individual or community, or otherwise by a series of events leading up to that moment of choice, of final decision. It is both a moment of judgement and of grace. It is a moment of suffering and of hope.

Such a moment arrived in my own life on March 21, 1960, the day of Sharpeville, when sixty-nine people protesting peacefully against the unjust pass laws of the apartheid regime, were shot and killed outside the police station of Sharpeville. That time was preceded in my life by a series of events and experiences leading up to that moment when God himself decided, now is the moment

112

when you've got to make your decision, either stand by your deepest convictions of what is right and true and loving, or forever be pushed aside. Such a moment I believe has arrived in the life of South Africa today. The *kairos*, the moment of truth for apartheid—as a regime and as a policy—evil, immoral, unjust, having had its day, as well as the *kairos* for the church.

A series of events led up to this moment of *kairos* which I believe is facing our whole country today. Starting possibly with Soweto in 1976, when from the midst of the hearts of thousands of young black students came the cry to say, "We are no longer prepared to accept this inferior and unjust and discriminatory system of Bantu education. We are going to unshackle these chains." Between six and seven hundred of them over South Africa died as a result of those protests which they set about.

A second step in that moment of *kairos* for our country was in November of 1983, when sixty-six percent of all whites of South Africa voluntarily decided to support in a referendum the new constitution which gave limited rights to the so-called Coloured and the Indian community, while excluding in principle every black citizen of South Africa from the whole process of political decision-making in our country, thereby the white community telling the black community of South Africa, "You are no part of us. You've never been part of us, and you will never be part of us."

Such a moment, another step in that crisis in the *kairos* of the country from which I come, and which I deeply love, came on the 3rd September, 1984, when seven thousand troops of the army moved into black townships of Sebokeng and Sharpeville, surrounding these townships late on the previous evening—and searching every single home, stamping every person with a dye so that it could be seen if he or she left the township that he/she had been identified by the police. And when the next morning came, the people of Sharpeville and Sebokeng said, "The government of this country has declared war on us."

Such a moment came, and I think perhaps brought it to the climax on the 21st of July this year, when the government declared a state of emergency in 36 magisterial districts of the country out of 285, in order to try and quell the unrest, bring back the country to so-called law and order, and the protesting, resisting masses into submission.

And [this is a] government which claims to be—proudly claims to be—Christian, claims to be the strongest anti-communist force on the continent of Africa, defending the values of Christianity and of civilization in the name of apartheid: is it any wonder that millions of those on the side of the oppressed, including millions of Christians, have said, "If this is what Christianity is about, then we wish to have nothing to do with it."

On Thursday I received a telex from the South African Council of Churches listing some of the men of the sixty who had been arrested in Cape Town, among them the names of well-known clergy . . . . And my first reaction was, because practically all of them are known to me, close friends, my first reaction was, "Oh God. Is this what is to happen?" And then upon reflection, immediately came the thought: perhaps it was good, perhaps it is necessary that more and more of us as Christians, as church leaders, that we should be behind bars and that behind bars we can proclaim and we can give our testimony—more meaningfully, more relevant, more potent and more powerful than remaining technically and formally free, but part of a situation which has become intolerable. It is the agony of the Christians. And that agony will continue, and it will deepen.

—Beyers Naudé
from a talk given at Riverside Church in New York
City, October 27, 1985

South Africa's people will be free

Many of you have asked me, and the press here continually ask me, but what about you? Aren't you afraid to go home? What will happen to you if you go home? Well, I have stood at the graveside of brave people, marvelous men and women and children who have given their lives for the struggle because they believed in it. I was at a funeral in South Africa on Saturday and I boarded the plane on Sunday to be back at this meeting to speak to you tonight. But I must ask you, my brother and sisters, do not be concerned for me. Because in my country much more is at stake than simply the life of one man. Be concerned for all those nameless little people who have no protection, whose names are not known, who will die tomorrow and no newspaper will even write one single word about them. They are the true brave people who have carried the flag for freedom in South Africa for many, many years without a single word of recognition from the world.

I have had my recognition and you will know when I die. But as I said to my people back home, I will say to you: If I die tomorrow, do not mourn me, and do not come to my funeral and sing freedom songs if while I am alive you were not willing to participate with us in the struggle for freedom and justice.

But I assure you tonight, and I say this from the bottom of my heart because among the many things that I am uncertain of in

South Africa, among the many things that I do not know anything about—I do not know what will happen tomorrow; I do not know what will happen to my family, I do not know what will happen to our people. One thing I know: South Africa's people shall be free! It is something that I have seen, it is something that I have experienced in the determination of young people who are no longer afraid to go out on the streets and face the dogs, and the tear gas, and the guns. I have seen this in the faces of our own people who have come alive again. I am strengthened again. I am encouraged again. I have hope again. South Africa's people will be free.

> —Allan Boesak
> from a speech at the National Urban League,
> July 1985

Three selections from the Kairos Document.

The moment of truth

The time has come. The moment of truth has arrived. South Africa has been plunged into a crisis that is shaking the foundations and there is every indication that the crisis has only just begun and that it will deepen and become even more threatening in the months to come. It is the *kairos*, or moment of truth, not only for apartheid but also for the church and all other faiths and religions.

We as a group of theologians have been trying to understand the theological significance of this moment in our history. It is serious, very serious. For very many Christians in South Africa this is the *kairos*, the moment of grace and opportunity, the favorable time in which God issues a challenge to decisive action. It is a dangerous time because, if this opportunity is missed and allowed to pass by, the loss for the church, for the gospel, and for all the people of South Africa will be immeasurable. Jesus wept over Jerusalem. He wept over the tragedy of the destruction of the city and the massacre of the people that was imminent, "and all because you did not recognize your opportunity *(kairos)* when God offered it" (Luke 19:44).

Tyranny and the Christian tradition

There are indeed some differences of opinion in the Christian tradition about the means that might be used to replace a tyrant *but* there has not been any doubt about our Christian duty to refuse to cooperate with any tyranny and to do whatever we can to remove it.

... There are conflicts that can only be described as the struggle between justice and injustice, good and evil, God and the devil. To speak of reconciling these two is not only a mistaken application of the Christian idea of reconciliation, it is a total betrayal of all that Christian faith has ever meant. Nowhere in the Bible or in Christian tradition has it ever been suggested that we ought to try to reconcile good and evil, God and the Devil. We are supposed to do away with evil, injustice, oppression and sin—not come to terms with it. We are supposed to oppose, confront and reject the devil and not try to sup with the devil.

It would be quite wrong to try to preserve "peace" and "unity" at all costs, even at the cost of truth and justice and, worse still, at the cost of thousands of young lives. As disciples of Jesus we should rather promote truth and justice and life at all costs, even at the cost of creating conflict, disunity, and dissension along the way. To be truly biblical our church leaders must adopt a theology that millions of Christians have already adopted—a biblical theology of direct confrontation with the forces of evil rather than a theology of reconciliation with sin and the devil.

A message of hope

... At the very heart of the gospel of Jesus Christ and at the very center of all true prophecy is a message of hope. Jesus has taught us to speak of this hope as the coming of God's kingdom. We believe that God is at work in our world turning hopeless and evil situations to good so that God's Kingdom may come and will may be done on earth as it is in heaven. We believe that goodness and justice and love will triumph in the end and that tyranny and oppression cannot last forever. One day "all tears will be wiped away" (Revelation 7:17; 12:4) and "the lamb will lie down with the lion" (Isaiah 11:6). True peace and true reconciliation are not only desirable, they are assured and guaranteed. This is our faith and our hope. We believe in and hope for the resurrection.

... As the crisis deepens day by day, what both the oppressor and the oppressed can legitimately demand of the churches is a message of hope. Most of the oppressed people of South Africa today and especially the youth do have hope. They are acting courageously and fearlessly because they have a sure hope that liberation will come. Often enough their bodies are broken, but nothing can now break their spirit. But hope needs to be confirmed. Hope needs to be maintained and strengthened. Hope needs to be spread. The people need to hear it said again and again that God is with them and that "the hope of the poor is never brought to nothing" (Psalm 9:18).

116

12. A Vision of the Future

In 1955, a gathering of three thousand representatives from the African National Congress, the South African Indian Congress, the Coloured People's Congress and the Congress of Democrats (a white group) spelled out clearly their vision of the future in their endorsement of the Freedom Charter. This is a document that has stood the test of time. During the last five years, particularly through the United Democratic Front, the Freedom Charter has again emerged as the expression of the binding vision of people of different races. Supported by many church leaders, it is consistent with the gospel challenge: "Whatever you wish that people would do to you, do so to them; for this is the law and the prophets" (Matthew 7:12). A choral reading of the Freedom Charter is at the heart of this final session.

Ritual

Jesus often referred to the kingdom of heaven as a great feast. Because this is the last session in this series of readings and prayers about South Africa, it is appropriate to close with an agape feast— a potluck supper to which each person brings a delicious dish. This is also a time to invite guests, particularly people of other races or cultures so that the gathering itself can be a foretaste of the final feast when people from every race and tribe and tongue gather together—the very opposite of all that apartheid stands for.

Encourage the regular members of the gathering to prepare for this session by re-establishing unity and trust in any relationships that have been broken.

Here is a suggested order for the occasion:

Introduction of guests
Explanation of theme

117

Potluck supper
Gospel reading: Luke 14:12-24
Reading of poems
Dramatic reading of "A Dream in the Desert"
Reading of "Today's Wish"
Reading of "Tomorrow's Sun"
Choral reading of the Freedom Charter
Listen to or sing freedom songs, ending with "O Freedom" or "Nkosi Sikelil'i Afrika," the South African hymn that has become the real national anthem

Final blessing: God bless Africa
Guard her children
Guide her rulers
And give her peace
For Jesus' sake. Amen

Readings

Vision of Peace

You stood at the center of a cloud,
Your hands outstretched like a forest,
Your warm face visible from the circular edge
Of a broken valley.
Playing children ran beside you,
They danced for the rebirth of your seasons.
Yes, it is children who die in wars.
Their minds molded for death, they sing the songs of death.
They sing the songs of war.
They imitate the footsteps of the soldier.
They declaim the poems of greatness.
Peace has cured me of all bitter memories
It has filled the mountain-cave with wisdom,
It has nourished life with a happy dream.
Knowledge comes from a state of awakening.
It is embedded in the softness of the vision.
We must repent. We must sing of life.
The lightning eye bores into the earth,
The children have arrived.
From them we must learn to create the unending movement.

By their birth we must swim through the turbulence like a bird.
Our peace is born from their innocence.
It is a song that praises the earth.

—Mazisi Kunene
from the *Ancestors and the Sacred Mountain*

No Screams Ring Forever

no screams ring forever
nor does pain last forever
something will always be done
the night knows this
this night which makes a day
which goes to make the night
giving way to the dawn
it winked and winked
long ago
it winks and winks now
as we design our day
and the day designs us
and new men and women are born
who mourn and bury the dead
who know the price of freedom
and say so
by knowing how to build new countries
where people work and eat
where people will become
like fruits
from roots which spread and spread
in the mind
the heart of a people
who learn science
who harness energy
who pit themselves against thirst and hunge
where everyone will read and write
where man child and woman are eager to learn
not to oppress

or exploit one another
where the day and the night
unfold.

—Mongane Serote
from *The Night Keeps Winking*

Their Love

We include this short love poem because so many people, including married couples, are separated from those they love by the laws of apartheid. In the future, those who love each other will be able to be together.

Such was the joy of their love:
Like sunrays cutting through the evening forest
Like a cluster of white cranes circling the horizon
Like twins whispering to each other
Like a gigantic mountain thrust against the sky
Like happy crowds assembled for the festival
Like a beautiful vessel kneaded by young girls
Like a gift of friendship before a long journey
Like mists, dangling low over the earth. . .

—Mazisi Kunene
from *The Ancestors and the Sacred Mountain*

Waiting

A Dream in the Desert

Olive Schreiner was a remarkable white woman who grew up on an isolated farm in the Cape in the nineteenth century. A hundred years ago she advocated both women's rights and African rights. Though the story included here focuses on the relationship between women and men "in the future," it pays tribute to all those who have helped make a track to the water's edge in the journey to the land of freedom, even those who were swept away and are heard of no more, and it is fitting that on this last day we honor them too.

(This should be read by three different readers. N = Narrator, R = Reason, W = Woman)

N: I saw a desert and I saw a woman coming out of it. And she came to the bank of a dark river; and the bank was steep and high. And on it an old man met her, who had a long white beard; and a stick that curled was in his hand, and on it was written Reason. And he asked her what she wanted; and she said,

W: "I am woman, and I am seeking for the land of Freedom."

R: "It is before you."

W: "I see nothing before me but a dark flowing river and a bank steep and high, and cuttings here and there with heavy sand in them."

R: "And beyond that?"

W: "I see nothing, but sometimes, when I shade my eyes with my hand, I think I see on the further banks trees and hills, and the sun shining on them!"

R: "That is the land of Freedom."

W: "How am I to get there?"

R: "There is but one way, and one only. Down the banks of Labor, through the water of Suffering. There is no other."

W: "There is no bridge?"

R: "None."

W: "Is the water deep?"

R: "Deep."

W: "Is the floor worn?"

R: "It is. Your foot may slip at any time, and you may be lost."

121

W: "Have any crossed already?"

R: "Some have tried!"

W: "Is there a track to show where the best fording is?"

R: "It has to be made."

N: She shaded her eyes with her hand;

W: "I will go."

R: "You must take off the clothes you wore in the desert: they are dragged down by them who go into the water so clothed."

N: And she threw from her gladly the mantle of Ancient-received-opinions she wore for it was worn full of holes. And she took the girdle from her waist that she had treasured so long, and the moths flew out of it in a cloud.

R: "Take the shoes of dependence off your feet."

N: And she stood there naked, but for one white garment that clung close to her.

R: "That you may keep. So they wear clothes in the Land of Freedom. In the water it buoys one up, it always swims."

N: And I saw on its breast was written Truth; and it was white; the sun had not often shone on it; the other clothes had covered it up.

R: "Take this stick; hold it fast. In that day when it slips from your hand you are lost. Put it down before you; feel your way: where it cannot find a bottom do not set your foot."

W: "I am ready, let me go."

R: "No—but stay; what is that—in your breast?"

N: And she was silent.

R: "Open it, and let me see."

N: And she opened it. And against her breast was a tiny thing, who drank from it, and the curls above his forehead pressed against it, and his knees were drawn up to her, and he held her breast fast with his hands.

R: "Who is he, and what is he doing here?"

W: "See his little wings."

R: "Put him down."

W: "He is asleep, and he is drinking! I will carry him to the Land

122

of Freedom. He has been a child so long, so long, I have carried him. In the land of Freedom he will be a man. We will walk together there, and his great white wings will overshadow me. He has lisped one word only to me in the desert—'Passion!' I have dreamed he might learn to say 'Friendship' in that land."

R: "Put him down!"

W: "I will carry him, so—with one arm, and with the other I will fight the water."

R: "Lay him down on the ground. When you are in the water you will forget to fight, you will think only of him. Lay him down." *(pause)* "He will not die. When he finds you have left him alone he will open his wings and fly. He will be in the Land of Freedom before you. Those who reach the Land of Freedom, the first hand they see stretching down the bank to help shall be Love's. He will be a man then, not a child. In your breast he cannot thrive; put him down that he may grow."

N: And she took her bosom from his mouth, and he bit her, so that blood ran down on to the ground. And she laid him down on the earth; and she covered her wound. And she bent and stroked his wings. And I saw the hair on her forehead turned white as snow, and she had changed from youth to age. And she stood far off on the bank of the river.

W: "For what do I go to this far land which no one has ever reached? Oh, I am alone! I am utterly alone!"

R: "Silence! What do you hear?"

N: And she listened intently,

W: "I hear the sound of feet, a thousand times ten thousand and thousands and thousands, and they beat this way!"

R: "They are the feet of those that shall follow you. Lead on! Make a track to the water's edge! Where you stand now, the ground will be beaten flat by ten thousand times ten thousand feet." And he said, "Have you seen the locusts, how they cross a stream? First one comes down to the water's edge; it is swept away, and then another comes and then another, and then another, and at last with their bodies piled up a bridge is built and the rest pass over."

W: "And of those who come first, some are swept away, and are heard of no more; their bodies do not even build the bridge?"

R: "And are swept away, and are heard of no more—and what

123

of that?"

W: "And what of that?"

R: "They make a track to the water's edge."

W: "They make a track to the water's edge." *(pause)* "Over that bridge which shall be built with our bodies, who will pass?"

R: "The entire human race."

N: And the woman grasped her staff.
And I saw her turn down that dark path to the river.
And I dreamed a dream.
I dreamed I saw a land. And on the hills walked brave women and brave men, hand in hand. And they looked into each other's eyes, and they were not afraid.
And I saw the women also hold each other's hands.
And I said to him beside me, "What place is this?"

R: "This is heaven."

N: "Where is it?"

R: "On earth."

N: "When shall these things be?"

R: "IN THE FUTURE."

> —Olive Schreiner
> from *Track to the Water's Edge.*

Tomorrow's Sun

Tomorrow's sun shall rise and it shall flood these dark kopjies* with light, and the rocks shall glint in it. Not more certain is that rising than the coming of the day. . . . Here on the spot where now we stand shall be raised a temple. People shall not gather in it to worship that which divides; but they shall stand in it shoulder to shoulder, white with black and the stranger with the inhabitant of the land; and the place shall be holy for all shall say, "Are we not brothers and sisters and the sons and daughters of one God?"

> —Olive Schreiner
> quoted in *Side by Side*

* Small rocky outcroppings

Today's Wish

Let the great gates open
And all the beautiful ones appear hand in hand
Let the morning embrace their feet with dew
Let all the simple joys sing the song of the dove
May we forgive those who have caused us pain;
For today only.

So that we may begin a new era
Riding high on the shoulders of the hill.
May we, as a final gift of life,
Hear voices shouting our poems
May we hear our children humming our anthems.
For it is said: a parent deserted by her children
Never finds the great gate to the earth.

> —Mazisi Kunene
> from *The Ancestors and the Sacred Mountain*

The Freedom Charter

Provide copies so that all can join in the reading of the Charter.

All: We, the people of South Africa, declare for all our country and the world to know:

1: That our people have been robbed of their birthright to land, liberty and peace by a form of government founded on injustice and ineqality;

2: That our country will never be prosperous or free until all our people live in brotherhood, enjoying equal rights and opportunities;

3: That only a democratic state, based on the will of all the people, can secure to all their birthright without distinction of color, race, sex, or belief;

All: And therefore, we the people of South Africa, black and white, together—equals, countrymen and brothers—adopt this Freedom Charter. And we pledge ourselves to strive together, sparing nothing of our strength and courage, until the democratic changes here set out have been won.

All: THE PEOPLE SHALL GOVERN:

1: Every man and woman shall have the right to vote for and stand as a candidate for all bodies which make laws;

2: All the people shall be entitled to take part in the administration of the country;

3: The rights of the people shall be the same regardless of race, color, or sex;

4: All bodies of minority rule, advisory boards, councils and authorities shall be replaced by democratic organs of self-government.

All: ALL NATIONAL GROUPS SHALL HAVE EQUAL RIGHTS:

1: There shall be equal status in the bodies of state, in the courts, and in the schools, for all national groups;

2: All people shall have equal rights to use their own language and to develop their own folk culture and customs;

3: All national groups shall be protected by law against insults to their race and nationality;

4: The preaching and practice of national, race or color discrimination and contempt shall be a punishable crime;

5: All apartheid laws and practices shall be set aside.

All: THE PEOPLE SHALL SHARE IN THE COUNTRY'S WEALTH:

1: The national wealth of our country, the heritage of all South Africans, shall be restored to the people;

2: The mineral wealth beneath the soil, the banks and monopoly industries shall be transferred to the ownership of the people as a whole;

3: All other industries and trade shall be controlled to assist the well-being of the people;

4. All people shall have equal rights to trade where they choose, to manufacture and to enter all trades, crafts, and professions.

All: THE LAND SHALL BE SHARED AMONG THOSE WHO WORK IT:

1: Restrictions of land ownership on a racial basis shall be ended, and all the land re-divided among those who work it, to banish famine and land hunger;

2: The state shall help the peasants with implements, seeds, tractors, and dams to save soil and assist the tillers;

3: Freedom of movement shall be guaranteed to all who work on the land;

4: All shall have the right to occupy land wherever they choose;

5: People shall not be robbed of their cattle, and forced labor and farm prisons shall be abolished.

All: ALL SHALL BE EQUAL BEFORE THE LAW:

1: No one shall be imprisoned, deported or restricted without a fair trial;

2: No one shall be condemned by the order on any government official;

3: The courts shall be representative of the people;

4: Imprisonment shall be only for serious crimes against people, and shall aim at re-education, not vengeance;

5: All laws which discriminate on grounds of race, color, or belief shall be repealed.

All: ALL SHALL ENJOY EQUAL HUMAN RIGHTS:

1: The law shall guarantee to all their right to speak, to organize, to meet together, to publish, to preach, to worship, and to educate their children;

2: The privacy of the house from police shall be protected by the law;

3: All shall be free to travel without restriction from countryside to town, from province to province, and from South Africa abroad;

4: Pass laws, permits and all other laws restricting these freedoms shall be abolished;

All: THERE SHALL BE WORK AND SECURITY:

1: All who work shall be free to form trade unions, to elect their officers and to make wage agreements with their employers;

2: The state shall recognize the right and duty of all to work and to draw full unemployment benefits;

3: Men and women of all races shall receive equal pay for equal work;

4: There shall be a forty-hour working week, a national minimum wage, paid annual leave, and sick leave for all workers, and maternity leave on full pay for all working mothers;

5: Miners, domestic workers, farm workers and civil servants shall have the same rights as all others who work;

6: Child labor, compound labor, the tot system and contract labor shall be abolished.

All: THE DOORS OF LEARNING AND OF CULTURE SHALL BE OPENED:

1: The government shall discover, develop and encourage national talent for the enhancement our our cultural life;

2: All the cultural treasures of mankind shall be open to all, by free exchange of books, ideas and contact with other lands;

3: The aim of education shall be to teach the youth to love their people and their culture, to honor human brotherhood, liberty and peace;

4: Education shall be free, compulsory, universal and equal for all children;

5: Higher education and technical training shall be opened to all by means of state allowances and scholarships awarded on the basis of merit;

6: Adult illiteracy shall be ended by a mass state education plan;

7: Teachers shall have all the rights of other citizens;

8: The color bar in cultural life, in sport and in education shall be abolished.

All: THERE SHALL BE HOUSES, SECURITY AND COMFORT:

1: All people shall have the right to live where they choose, to be decently housed, and to bring up their families in comfort and security;

2: Unused housing space to be made available to the people;

3: Rent and prices shall be lowered, food plentiful and no one shall go hungry;

4: A preventative health scheme shall be run by the state;

5: Free medical care and hospitalization shall be provided for all, with special care for mothers and young children;

6: Slums shall be demolished, and new suburbs built where all have transport, roads, lighting, playing fields, creches and social centers;

7: The aged, the orphans, the disabled and the sick shall be cared for by the state;

8: Rest, leisure and recreation shall be the right of all;

9: Fenced locations and ghettos shall be abolished, and laws which break up families shall be repealed.

All: THERE SHALL BE PEACE AND FRIENDSHIP:

1: South Africa shall be a fully independent state which respects the rights and sovereignty of all nations;

2: South Africa shall strive to maintain world peace and the settlement of all international disputes by negotiations—not war;

3: Peace and friendship among all our people shall be secured by upholding the equal rights, opportunities and status of all;

4: The people of the protectorates—Basutoland, Bechuanaland and Swaziland—shall be free to decide for themselves their own future;

5: The right of all the people of Africa to independence and self-government shall be recognized, and shall be the basis of close cooperation.

All: Let all who love their people and their country now say, as we say here:

"THESE FREEDOMS WE WILL FIGHT FOR, SIDE BY SIDE, THROUGHOUT OUR LIVES, UNTIL WE HAVE WON OUR LIBERTY."

RESOURCES

Photographs

Portrait of a People, by Eli Weinberg. International Defense and Aid Fund (IDAF), P.O. Box 17, Cambridge, MA 02138, or P.O. Box 1034, Station B, Ottawa, Ontario Kl P 54L. The following are also available from IDAF in book form or as sets of display photographs: The Struggle is My Life: Nelson Mandela; Women Under Apartheid; Children Under Apartheid.

South Africa, The Cordoned Heart: Twenty South African Photographers, New York and London: W.W. Norton and Co., 1986. Summary of a poverty study by Francis Wilson. Excellent photographs.

Letter to Farzanah, by Omar Badsha. Institute for Black Research, P.O. Box 37315, Overport, Durban, 4067 South Africa. Excellent photographs of children.

Working Women: A Portrait of South Africa's Black Woman Worker. Johannesburg: Sached Trust, Ravan Press, P.O. Box 31134, Braamfontein, 2017 South Africa.

Audiovisuals

"No Middle Road to Freedom." 1/2" VHS, 45 min.
A history of the African National Congress and a look at the fate of the movement's jailed leader, Nelson Mandela.
Rental from EcuFilm, 810 12th Avenue South, Nashville, TN 37203. Tel: 800-251-4091.

The following are also available from EcuFilm:

"Land of Fear, Land of Courage." 1/2" VHS, 60 min.
Anglican Archbishop Desmond Tutu discusses the time bomb of racial politics. Narrated by Edwin Newman.

"South Africa Belongs to Us." 16mm film, 35 min.
An intimate portrait of five typical South African women, demonstrating the emotional and economic burdens borne by families under apartheid.

"Witness to Apartheid." 16 mm film, 56 min.
The victims of daily police terrorism in South Africa call out to the world in this unforgettable documentary.

Note also the Friendship Press video and filmstrip described on the inside back cover of this book.

For additional titles of audiovisuals on South Africa, contact: Southern Africa Media Center, California Newsreel, 630 Natoma Street, San Francisco, CA 94103. Tel: 415-621-6196.

Recordings

Rain Upon Dry Land, by Carolyn McDade. Cassette. Includes the song, "You have touched the woman, you have struck a rock," composed for the women's protest described on page 71. Available for $7.00 (plus $2.00 postage and handling) from the Womancenter at Plainville, 76 Everett Skinner Rd., Plainville, MA, 02762. Tel: 617-699-7167.

Also available from the same address: *This Tough-Spun Web,* testimony of South African women. $15.00 for set that includes cassette and reflection-action songbook.

The following are available from: Sikhulu Record Shack, Inc., 274 West 125th Street, New York, NY 10027. Tel: 212-866-1600.

Sarafina, the Broadway musical from South Africa, includes Zulu-style choral singing and *mbaqanga,* which blends Western pop sound with unmistakeably African melodies. (Shanachie 43052, LP, cassette and CD)

Sangoma, Miriam Makeba's newest album includes ancient Zulu and Xhosa songs; liner notes explain how these songs are parables, ceremonies and carriers of history. (Warner Bros. 25673, LP, cassette and CD)

Let Their Voices Be Heard, an album of traditional South African music includes songs recorded at churches, homes and parties; listen for a trio of nurses delivering nutritional advice in harmony. (Rounder 5024, LP and cassette)

Mbube, an all-night singing competition recorded at a miners' hostel in Durban; precise, robust call-and-response singing from the Zulu tradition, gospel hymns and 1950s rock-and-roll. (Rounder 5023)

Thunder Before Dawn. (Virgin 90866-1)

Imala, by Ladysmith Black Mambazo. (Shanachie 43040)

The Indestructable Beat of Soweto, Vols. 1 and 2. (Shanachie 43033)

Rhythm of Resistance: Music of Black South Africa. (Shanachie 43018)

LIST OF SOURCES WITH INDEX

Biko, Steve. *I Write What I Like*. London: Heinemann Educational Books, Ltd., 1978.

A definition of black consciousness, 48; Steve Biko challenges church priorities, 107.

Boesak, Allan. "South Africa's people will be free." Excerpt from a speech given at the National Urban League, 114.

Brink, Andre and J.M. Coetzee, eds. *A Land Apart: A Contemporary South African Reader*. New York: Viking Penguin, 1986.

Wednesday, 18 August 1976, 17.

Brutus, Dennis. *Letters to Martha and Other Poems* (No. 46 of the African Writers Series). London: Heinemann Educational Books, Ltd., 1968.

A Poem Written from Prison on Robben Island, 93.

Bryan, George McLeod. *Naudé: Prophet to South Africa*. Atlanta: John Knox Press, 1978.

The task of reconciliation, 40.

Chapman, Michael and Achmat Dangor, eds. *Voices from Within*. Johannesburg: Ad. Donker Pty. Ltd., 1982.

Possibilities for a Man Hunted by SBs, 31; Death, 33; White Lies, 50.

Couzens, Kim and Essop Patel, eds. *The Return of the Aamasi Bird*. Johannesburg: Ravan Press, 1982.

An Agony, 100.

deGruchy, John. *Cry Justice!* Maryknoll, NY: Orbis Press, 1986.

Freedom via the Cross, 38.

Feinberg, Barry, ed. *Poets to the People: South African Freedom Poems*. London: Heinemann Educational Books, Ltd., 1980.

I Am the Exile, 30; Manifesto, 53; Lilian Ngoyi, 73; And I Watch It in Mandela, 86.

Frederikse, Julie. *South Africa: A Different Kind of War*. Johannesburg: Ravan Press, 1986.

An inspiration, 66.

Gray, Stephen, ed. *Modern South African Poetry*. Johannesburg: Ad. Donker Pty. Ltd., 1984.

The Whiteman Blues, 97.

Hope, Marjorie and James Young. *The South African Churches in a Revolutionary Situation*. Maryknoll, NY: Orbis Press, 1983.

Archbishop Hurley speaks of his involvement in protest, 108; Allan Boesak on choosing to be black, 110.

The International Herald Tribune, June 30, 1987.

Ten thousand children detained in 1986 "emergency", 94.

Joseph, Helen. *Side by Side*. New York: William Morrow & Co., 1986.

The school boycott continues, 18; The signing of the Freedom Charter at the congress at Kliptown, 1955, 26; A visit to Chief Luthuli in banishment, 30; The Alexandra bus boycotts, 1943 and 1944, 39; Twenty thousand strong we marched. . ., 71; The tie of friendship, 73; Lilian's death, 75; A strange married life, 82; The horror of detention, 83; Women prisoners in the Johannesburg "Fort", 92; The privilege and pain of being white, 98; Tomorrow's Sun, 124.

Kameeta, Zephania. *Why, O Lord? Psalms and Sermons from Namibia*. Geneva: World Council of Churches, 1986.

Psalm 126, *dedication page.*

Komai, Felicia. *Cry, The Beloved Country* (a verse drama based on Alan Paton's novel). New York: Friendship Press, 1954.

The Politician and the Priest, 24.

Kunene, Daniel P. *A Seed Must Seem to Die.* Johannesburg: Ravan Press, 1981.

The Soweto Child, 3; Solar Power, 8; Soweto, 9. Warrior, 16; Living is Forever, 56; Do Not Ask Me, 65.

Kunene, Mazisi. *The Ancestors and the Sacred Mountain.* London: Heinemann Educational Books, 1982.

The Children Have Arrived, 13; The Rise of the Angry Generation, 15; Motherhood, 59; Nozizwe, 100; Vision of Peace, 118; Their Love, 120; Today's Wish, 125.

Kuzwayo, Ellen. *Call Me Woman.* San Francisco: Spinsters/Aunt Lute Book Co. (223 Mississippi, P.O. Box 410687, San Francisco, CA 94141), 1985.

Memories of Steve, 47; Making pots, 60; The experience of black nannies when they grow old, 62; An unexpected visitor, 76; Sowing seeds of mistrust, 98.

Logan, Willis H. ed. *The Kairos Covenant: Standing with South African Christians.* New York: Friendship Press; Oak Park, IL: Meyer-Stone Books, 1988.

Three selections from the Kairos Document, 115.

Malibongwe. London: African National Congress Women.

Masechaba, 49; Childhood in Soweto, 51.

Mandela, Nelson. *The Struggle is My Life.* New York: Pathfinder Press, 1986.

Nelson Mandela at the Treason Trial, 40; Mandela's testimony, 1960, 41; The Rivonia Trial, 1962, 80; Mandela's confidence, 84; Robben Island, 91.

Mandela, Nelson. "The birthright of the people." Excerpt from Mandela's response to President Botha's conditional offer of freedom, February 1985, 85.

Mandela, Winnie. *Part of My Soul Went with Him.* New York: W.W. Norton Co., 1985.

June 16, 1976, 15; Nelson's friends, 72; How can I lose hope? 81; Winnie's detention, 82; Liberated in prison, 83; The first contact visit, 84; The ANC is committed to non-racialism, 102.

The Message of Mahatma Gandhi. Publication Division, Government of India.

Nonviolence, 37.

Mtshali, Mbuyiseni Oswald. *Sounds of a Cowhide Drum.* Oxford: Oxford University Press, 1971.

The Shepherd and his Flock, 5; Boy on a Swing, 7.

Naude, Beyers. "Reflections on the Kairos Moment." Excerpt from a talk given at Riverside Church, 112.

Nolan, Albert and Richard Broderick. *To Nourish Our Faith: Theology of Liberation for Southern Africa.* Hilton, South Africa: The Order of Preachers (Southern Africa), 1987.

Kairos—The Moment of Truth, 111.

Olver, Frances M. M., ed. *The Oak and the Peach.* Johannesburg: Macmillan Publishing Co., 1984.

The African Pot, 61.

Paton, Alan. *Cry, The Beloved Country.* New York: Charles Scribner's Sons, 1948.

How shall we fashion a land of peace? 96.

Royston, Robert, ed. *To Whom It May Concern: An Anthology of Black South African Poetry.* Johannesburg: Ad. Donker, Pty. Ltd., 1973.

Mother's Ode to a Stillborn Child, *4*; I Will Wait, *6*; Naked They Come, *8*; Taken for a Ride, *25*; Ride Upon Death Chariot, *28*; The Pension Jiveass, *29*.

Schreiner, Olive. *A Track to the Water's Edge.* New York: Harper and Row, 1973.

A Dream in the Desert, *121*.

Serote, Mongane. *The Night Keeps Winking.* Gaborone, Botswana: Medu Art Ensemble, 1982.

Notes, *18*; Memories Don't Break Chains, *44*; The Chain Must Be Broken..., *54*; No Screams Ring Forever, *119*.

South Africa, The Cordoned Heart: Twenty South African Photographers. Capetown: Gallery Press; New York and London: W.W. Norton and Co., 1986.

The Child Who Was Shot Dead by Soldiers at Nyanga, *20*.

South Africa: Time is Running Out. Study Comission on U.S. Policy toward South Africa, Foreign Policy Study Foundation. Berkeley: University of California Press, 1981.

...as a human being, *96*.

Staffrider Magazine, Vol. 6, No. 3, 1986. Johannesburg: Ravan Press.

Black Mother, *62*; Knocks on the Door, *64*.

Voices of Women. New York: Women's International Resource Exchange, 1981.

Here I Stand, *67*.

Vukani Makhosikazi: South African Women Speak. London: Catholic Institute for International Relations. Undated.

The sharp end of the knife, *63*; Shopping, *64*; Bringing up kids in a prison cell, *92*.

Walshe, Peter. *Church versus State in South Africa: The Case of the Christian Institute.* Maryknoll, NY: Orbis Press, 1983.

Manas Buthelezi reverses mission, *109*.